Tarot

Tarot

Hali Morag

Astrolog Publishing House

Graphic Design: Ruth Erez
Cover Design: Na'ama Yaffe
Editor: Marion Duman
Production: Dan Gold

Astrolog Publishing House

P. O. Box 1123, Hod Hasharon 45111, Israel
Tel: 972-9-7412044
Fax: 972-9-7442714
E-mail: info@astrolog.co.il
Astrolog Web Site: www.astrolog.co.il

© Hali Morag 2002

ISBN 965-494-120-1

All rights reserved. No part of this publication may be reproduced, stored in a retrieval system, or transmitted, in any form or by any means, electronic, mechanical, photocopying, recording or otherwise, without the prior permission of the publisher.

Published by Astrolog Publishing House 2002

Illustrations from the Rider-Waite Tarot Deck©, known also as the Rider Tarot and the Waite Tarot, reproduced by permission of U.S. Games Systems, Inc., Stamford, CT 06902 USA. Copyright© 1971 by U.S. Games Systems, Inc. Further reproduction prohibited. The Rider-Waite Tarot Deck© is a registered trademark of U.S. Games Systems, Inc.

10 9 8 7 6 5 4 3 2 1

Contents

Introduction 7

The Major Arcana 15
    The Magician 16
    The High Priestess 18
    The Empress 20
    The Emperor 22
    The Hierophant 24
    The Lovers 26
    The Chariot 28
    Strength 30
    The Hermit 32
    Wheel of Fortune 34
    Justice 36
    The Hanged Man 38
    Death 40
    Temperance 42
    The Devil 44
    The Tower 46
    The Star 48
    The Moon 50
    The Sun 52
    Judgement 54
    The World 56
    The Fool 58

The Minor Arcana 61
    The Cups Suit from Ace to Page 64
    The Wands Suit from Ace to Page 77
    The Pentacles Suit from Ace to Page 90
    The Swords Suit from Ace to Page 115
    The Knight Cards 116

Examples of Spreads 121
    1 Should I Tell? 124
    2 Is This Just A Passing Crisis? 126
    3 Is She Sincere? 128
    4 Should I Start a Business? 130
    5 Will I Be Able to Pay? 132
    6 Who'll Get the Promotion? 134
    7 Will My Daughter Have a Transplant? 136
    8 How Long Have I Got To Live? 138
    9 Will My Daughter Leave Her Junkie Boyfriend? 140
   10 Trapped 142

Tips for Reading the Cards 145
    The List 146
    What it means when cards recur in spreads 173
    Arthur Waite's Tips 187

Introduction

The place of origin of playing cards in general and of Tarot cards in particular is uncertain, and speculations about this topic abound. At the beginning of the 12th century, hand-drawn cards appeared for the first time, and it was from these that the Tarot cards familiar to us today developed.

Tarot cards as we know them first appeared in northern Italy in the 14th century. They were used both for games and for mystical purposes, and later they developed into both the modern Tarot deck and the pack of playing cards used today.

The Tarot deck is divided into two sets: the Major Arcana and the Minor Arcana.

The Major Arcana consists of 22 picture cards. Twenty-one of them are numbered in ascending order, while one, The Fool, is either not numbered or it has a value of zero. The 22 cards parallel the 22 letters in the Hebrew alphabet.

The Minor Arcana consists of 56 cards, which are divided into four suits of 14 cards each: Swords, Wands, Cups and Pentacles. Each suit consists of ten numerological cards (from 1 to 10), three court cards (which are also known as family or royal cards), and one knight card. In other words, each suit comprises three "sub-suits." The entire Minor Arcana can therefore be divided into three sub-suits: 40 numerological cards, 12 court cards, and four knight cards.

Tarot cards were used for games, for predicting the future, and for teaching complicated mystical concepts. The Major Arcana presents a full symbolic method which was considered to be the key to the mystery and knowledge of the true nature of man, the universe and God. Kabbalistic, Gnostic, Neo-Platonic and other mystic influences can be discerned, all of which contributed to the design of the symbols that appear on the Tarot cards.

It is speculated that the origin of the cards is in China or India, and that they were introduced into Europe by gypsies. Another theory surmises that the cards were passed on from generation to generation as the sum of the knowledge of the 12th-century Kabbalists. Many people who deal with the occult believe that Tarot is the essence of ancient Egyptian wisdom.

Besides their being a vehicle for meditation and for instruction in mysticism and magic, Tarot cards are used broadly and comprehensively for predicting or guessing the future.

This book addresses readers who wish to familiarize themselves with Tarot cards in order to read cards, that is, for knowing the relevant information about the querent, his past, the forces that work on him, and most importantly, his future.

Arthur Edward Waite (1857-1942), an American who moved to England, was an expert in esoteric knowledge in the order known as the Golden Dawn. Waite created the new Tarot cards in conjunction with the painter, Pamela Coleman-Smith, in 1908. All 78 cards in this deck are illustrated with unique pictures, and every card contains special information. These Tarot cards, which are known as the Rider-Waite Tarot deck (Rider was the publisher of the cards), are the most renowned and commonly used cards in the world today.

Let us now take a look at reading or spreading the cards.

A great deal of intuition, imagination, diplomacy and tact are required for the actual act of reading; you have to use the different meanings that are offered for interpreting the cards as a basis that will guide you in reading the cards.

Beware of using the card-reading for negative purposes. You must remember that as a card-reader, you bear a lot of responsibility. People often take the prediction of their future far more seriously than they imagine.

If you discern death, illness, betrayal or failure in a spread, try to be as delicate and as tactful as possible in your interpretation. Always bear in mind that you may be wrong. Remember, too, that the basis of every interpretation is the knowledge of the special significance of each card.

When we are familiar with the meanings of the cards in the deck we have chosen, when we understand the significance of the cards and the connection between them, we must go through another stage before discussing the different spreads that determine the relationship between one card and another, as well as the interpretation given by the reader or the one who interprets the cards for the person who is consulting him.

This stage, which can be called "ambience," is valid for any deck we may choose to use — for the 22 cards of the Major Arcana, the 56 cards of the Minor Arcana — or the 78 cards in the complete deck, which consists of the Major and Minor Arcanas together.

Reading the cards helps us pick up the messages that the querent sends us, and we pick up the answers to the questions from one or other source. It is clear that if an irritable, short-tempered person sits down opposite us, we will immediately pick up his worried, tense messages. If a calm, relaxed person sits opposite us, the messages we will pick up will be entirely different.

In order to pick up the messages, the ambiance must be right — and that depends on four factors: the querent, the card-reader, the place and the cards used.

When the querent comes to a card reader, the latter must immediately assess the state he is in. There is no point making a reading the cards for a person who is in an state of either extreme agitation on the one hand or exaggerated complacency to the point of unconcealed contempt on the other. It just won't work!

When a person consciously declares that he does not believe in cards, this does not present an obstacle; however, if a person keeps on glancing at his watch and announcing that he does not have time, cancel the reading and make an appointment for another time.

It is important for the card-reader to understand immediately who he is dealing with. If you know the querent, you can explain to him that the ambiance is unsuitable. If he is unfamiliar, put him off gently for another time.

The same is true for the card-reader: If he feels that he is not on form — something is bothering him, for example, or he is tired or unfocused — he should put off the reading for another time.

As for the surroundings, it is important that the reading or the spread be performed in a quiet place, preferably when the querent and the reader are alone. A card-reader who relates to his profession seriously can give a superficial overview to the querent in a public place or on a stage — but the more profound interpretation will always take place in a quiet, modest location, with just the two of them.

The cards used by the reader must be in good condition, so that they inspire respect. It is customary to keep them wrapped up in fabric, preferably in a paper, wooden or leather box — never metal or plastic! The cards must be clean and whole.

The cards must be touched with clean hands only; many people habitually wash their hands before the reading. The table must be covered with a cloth, with no other objects on it. (Some readers, however, keep a crystal or gemstone on the table in order to eliminate negative energies from the surroundings.)

The card-reader is the only one who touches and shuffles the cards — no one else does! The shuffling of the cards is supposed to take about two minutes. During this time, the reader must concentrate on the querent opposite him — the querent always sits opposite the reader — and try to pick up his messages (even before the reading).

No matter what kind of reading, cards or spread you use, you must always go step by step, starting from the easy questions and gradually getting to the difficult, crucial ones.

Never deal with "irritating" or "provoking" questions! Bear in mind that the cards only show the way — but it is up to the querent to decide whether he will go along it!

The more information you have about the querent, the more accurate your answers will be. On the other hand, however, this information constitutes an energy blockage against the messages being sent by the querent! You must find the middle path between the information and the message, between the visible and the concealed. You will reach a balance only after a long period of cumulative experience.

When the tidings you have to impart are bad — illness, death, separation, loss, and so on — examine the cards a second time and think over and over again how to tell the querent the difficult answer or message.

Under no circumstances must you argue with the querent; the reader simply says what he sees in the cards. Period. The querent is free to accept or reject the answer.

Now that the ambiance is suitable, we are almost ready to begin understanding the cards, their interpretation and their significance in a spread. First, however, we have to discuss two additional points.

In the process of spreading the cards, it is important, mainly from the point of view of the ambiance, how the cards are shuffled and extracted before the "opening" of the particular spread.

The process is as follows:

- The querent enters the room, is received by the card reader, and sits down next to the table. The reader sits down at the opposite side of the table.
- The querent asks his question.
- The reader takes out his deck and shuffles them with his hands. (Make sure that all the cards are facing the same way.)
- The reader passes the deck to the querent, who continues to shuffle them. After a time, following the reader's instruction, he places the cards on the table face down.
- The reader halves the deck, places the upper half on the table, and places the lower half on top of it. This halving operation must be repeated three times.
- The reader takes the top card and places it facing upward in the position of card number one, and continues to extract the number of cards required for the spread (see page 113).
- Now, after the instructions have been followed, the spread is laid out in front of the reader — more precisely, on the table between him and the querent, and the interpretation can begin. At this point, we will say a few words about Tarot cards and numerology.

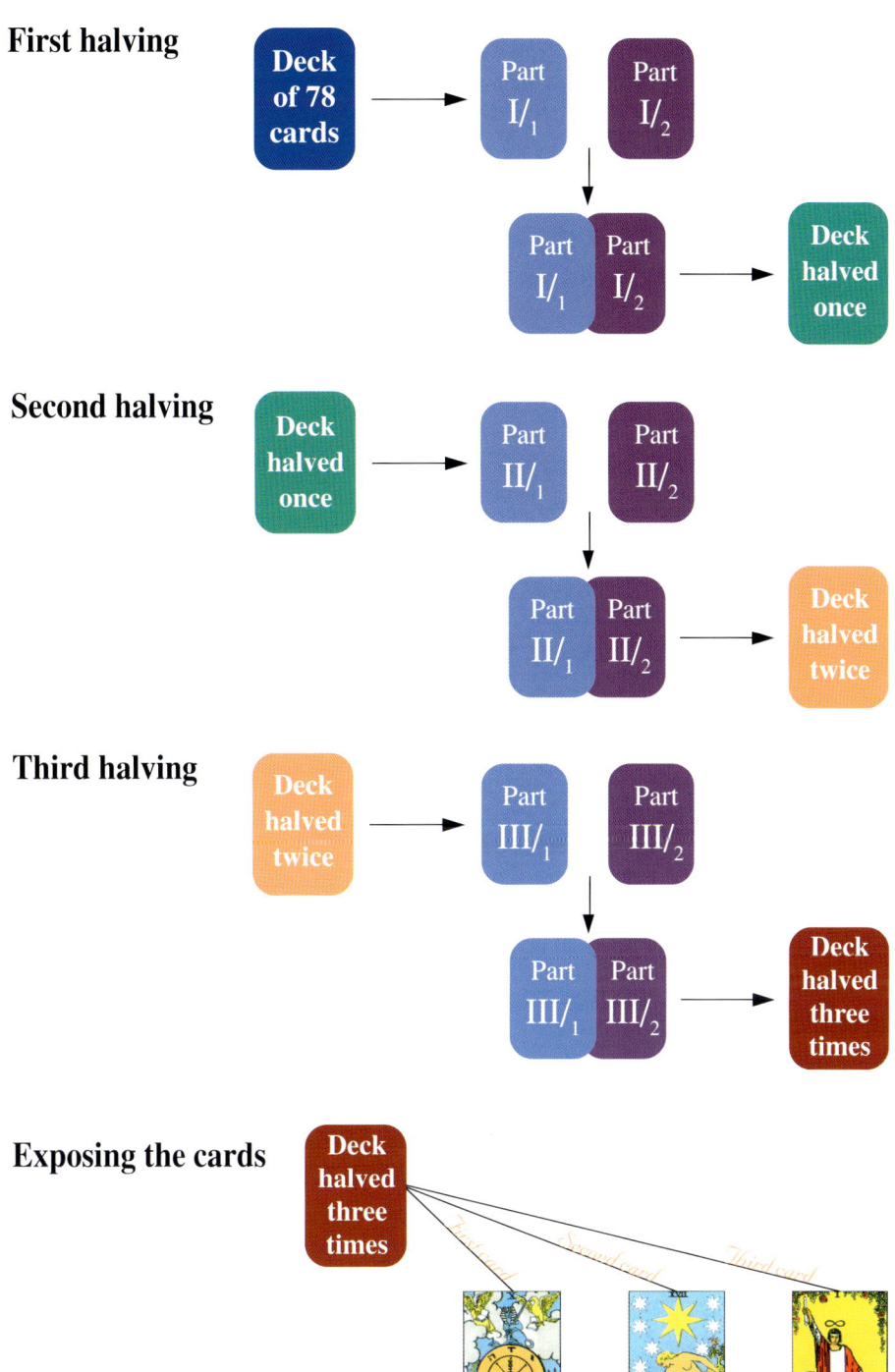

When we discuss the Minor Arcana of the Tarot deck, we must remember that most of the set — forty out of fifty-six cards — are cards with a pronounced numerological significance. There are four suits of cards, each containing cards numbered 1 to 10. Let us start off by pointing out that the number 10 is insignificant here, in its numerological analysis, since it is the card that realizes card number 9, and takes us back to card number 1 — that is, it unites the properties of the two cards/numbers mentioned above.

It is important to recall that numerology developed together with Tarot cards. In the centers of wisdom where the philosophy of Tarot cards was developed, the science of numerology developed as well.

Numerological interpretation is based on the Pythagorean theory: "Each number has its own force, which is not expressed merely in the form of the number or in its numerical expressions. This force derives from the occult connection that stems from the principles of nature that are expressed in numbers."

"The world is constructed on numbers," according to Pythagoras' theory. That is, all the phenomena in the world can be contained in the nine basic numbers.

The numerology of Tarot cards, in the most accepted version, is that of Cornelius Agrippa, and appeared in his book, "The Philosophy of Occultism" (1533). Card-readers tended to rely on those interpretations.

The numerological interpretation of the nine numbers is as follows:

Number 1: Purpose, vocation, aggressiveness, action, ambition. Like the letter A. The number is like an arrow aimed at a target.

Number 2: A antithetical number in which there are the extremes of day and night, and equilibrium by means of the combination of opposites.

Number 3: By means of the triangle, symbolizes the past, present and future. It is a number that "adapts itself."

Number 4: Stability and perseverance, indicated by a square, by the winds, the seasons, and the elements — fire, water, air, earth. A "primitive" number.

Number 5: Adventure, a "mobile" number that accumulates experience. Instability leads to uncertainty. An unpredictable number.

Number 6: Dependency. Harmony with nature. This number is amazingly balanced, being a combination of 2 and 3: 2x3=6, 6/3=2, 6/2=3.

Number 7: Mysterious, enables learning and knowledge to penetrate the unknown, the occult world. It represents the seven planets, the seven notes, the seven days of the week. It combines the perfection of 6 with the unity of 1, and this is where its spiritual power comes from.

Number 8: Material success. Double square. Divides into 4 and 4, or into 2 and 2 and 2 and 2, and this is where its stability comes from.

Number 9: "Absolute" success. The symbol of the universe. The biggest of the single-digit numbers. It bestows inspiration because of being 3x3.

Color Cards

In the last decade, humankind has been coming back to color. In ancient days, people — especially the sages, the religious teachers and the shamans — knew the importance of the colors. Red had a much broader meaning than the mere optical or chemical meaning of the composition of the color. The color had a mystical significance that played a role in rituals, spells, healing, and other fields of mind and spirit.

Today, there is a return to colors, and Tarot cards are also used as color cards.

Color cards are cards that are actually used for meditation. We look at a particular color card, take cognizance of its color (or lack of color), and, by means of inspiration and our ability to visualize, try to increase or decrease the property of the particular color in our body-mind-spirit.

Every one of the Tarot cards is defined as a color card containing one of two options: an *excess* of color in the card or a *lack* of color in the card. If we want to increase the absorption of the particular color, we select a Tarot card in which there is an excess of that color. If we want to decrease the absorption of the particular color, we select a Tarot card in which there is a lack of that color.

Tarot cards offer us an additional aspect of color cards — we can randomly choose a Tarot card out of the 78-card Tarot deck, and this Tarot card will indicate which color is present in us excessively, and which color is lacking in us.

In fact, in everyday practical use, we choose three Tarot cards, and place them from left to right, in a row.

The first card to be turned over (the left-hand card) indicates the past. That is, it answers the questions: "Which color affected me in the past more than all others?" (an excess of color). "Which color did I lack most of all?" (a lack of color).

The second card to be turned over (the middle card) relates to the present. That is, it answers the questions: "Which color affects me more than all others at present?" (an excess of color). "Which color am I lacking most of all at present?" (a lack of color).

The third card to be turned over (the right-hand card) relates to the future. That is, it answers the questions: "Which color must I increase in myself in the future?" (an excess of color). "Which color must I decrease in myself in the future?" (a lack of color).

Past	Present	Future
WHEEL of FORTUNE	 THE STAR	 THE MAGICIAN

It is obvious that the colors symbolize properties — properties of body, mind, or spirit. We will now present a brief summary of the properties of the seven colors that comprise the set of color cards.

Remember that the color, or its properties, can be excessive or lacking. That is, it is an axis whose one arm represents excess (+) and whose other arm represents lack (-), while its center point represents balance.

Excess (+)   Balance   (–) Lack

Purple — action, wisdom, connection to the cosmos, awareness, and enlightenment
Indigo — spiritual development, ability to think, capacity for inner balance
Blue — spiritual cleanliness, fecundity of thought, purity of heart, mental calmness
Green — creativity, growth, blooming, expansion, self-healing ability
Yellow — practicality, persistence, ability to accomplish (goals)
Orange — ability to control (body and mind), accomplishment of goals, link to earthiness
Red — self-confidence, self-focus, control of life, energy

In other words, if a person chooses a Tarot card in which there is an excess of red and a lack of blue, the meaning of the card is that he has excessive self-confidence but his spiritual cleanliness is not immaculate, and he has to repair whatever is in need of repair. If the Tarot card contains an excess of yellow and a lack of orange, the person is extremely practical in his behavior, but occasionally lacks the ability to control his actions.

Further on in the book, the lack and excess of colors in every Tarot card is indicated as an integral part of the card's properties.

The 78 Cards

The Major Arcana

The 22 cards of the Major Arcana appear here in great detail. The examples of the cards both here and in the Minor Arcana come from the Rider-Waite deck.

There is a detailed description of the card (including its symbols), and the meaning of the card when it is upright and in reverse.

The Magician 1

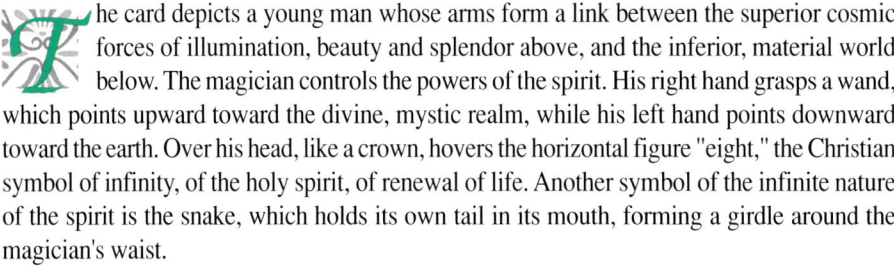

The main idea expressed in this card is

"You are holding all the cards in your hands."

Description

The card depicts a young man whose arms form a link between the superior cosmic forces of illumination, beauty and splendor above, and the inferior, material world below. The magician controls the powers of the spirit. His right hand grasps a wand, which points upward toward the divine, mystic realm, while his left hand points downward toward the earth. Over his head, like a crown, hovers the horizontal figure "eight," the Christian symbol of infinity, of the holy spirit, of renewal of life. Another symbol of the infinite nature of the spirit is the snake, which holds its own tail in its mouth, forming a girdle around the magician's waist.

In front of the magician, the four Tarot symbols are spread out on a table: the pentacle, with the mystical pentagram symbol on it, the cup, the wand, and the sword. These could also symbolize the four elements: fire, water, air and earth.

Under the table, an abundance of red roses and white lilies grow, symbols of divine inspiration. Part of the table is hidden — and that is an indication of the fact that man's knowledge is very limited.

In mythology, this card depicts the Greek god, Hermes, who could manipulate the lives of gods and mortals, and had the gift of being able to change his appearance and form at will, as well as of foreseeing and changing the future.

This card represents the divine spark in man — man's desire to unite with the Supreme Power. It is a masculine card, full of creative energy.

The card radiates success as a result of personal strength.

In a spread

The significance of the "Magician" card in a spread lies in the fact that it indicates great success in any field, with the querent in total control. He holds all the cards, so to speak, pulls the strings, and dictates the nature of any situation. The card characterizes doctors, lawyers, businessmen, magicians, and gamblers. It sometimes hints at a powerful person who either helps or hinders the querent, depending on its position in the spread. It also begins a new cycle, or hints at the beginning of a new cycle.

If the card appears **upright**, it represents will power, diplomacy, skill, a quest for heaven and earth. There are also negative characteristics such as disasters, losses and illness. You must exercise tact in the near future. It would be good for you to display your skills. Your self-confidence will serve you well.

If the card appears **in reverse**, it warns of confusion, disgrace, unrest, unrealized talent, illusion, the possibility of failure, and total failure. Watch out for situations that could lead to mental breakdowns and other illnesses.

Other important symbols contained in "The Magician" card:

1. The **raised hand** symbolizes the ability to absorb powers from the upper realms by means of magical knowledge (the magician's wand).
2. The **down-pointing hand** transfers the powers to the lower realm.
3. The **white color** of the robe and the lilies symbolizes purity and spirituality, while the **red color** of the robe and the roses symbolizes the physical, material realm.
4. The **symbol of infinity** implies divine protection.
5. The **snake** symbolizes magical strength and healing powers.

An excess of color		A lack of color	
	🟥		🟦

The High Priestess 2

The main idea expressed in this card is that of secrets,

secrecy, mystery and enigma.

Description

The High Priestess, wearing a two-horned crown with the Earth in the center, sits between the two columns of the mystical Temple, Boaz (the black column) and Jachin (the white one). Behind her hangs the temple curtain decorated with pomegranates and palm trees. At her feet lies a crescent moon, a symbol either of Islam or of idol-worship. The Cross of the Great Sun lies on her breast, and in her hands, partially concealed by the layers of her robe, is the Torah scroll, engraved with the word TORA, representing the wisdom of the world, eternal law, and great mystery — some of which is hidden from mere mortals. The contradictory symbols of the Torah, the cross, and the moon enhance the enigmatic nature of the card.

The colors in the card hint at light, brilliance, and an atmosphere of mystery. The High Priestess sits on the threshold of the Temple of Isis (the priestess of occult wisdom and priestess of the Hidden Church that unites God and man). She represents the "second marriage" of the prince who is no longer of this earth: she is the Holy Virgin, the spiritual bride, the mother, the daughter of the stars from the celestial Garden of Eden. She symbolizes the moon nursing at the breast of the supreme mother, who is the symbol of purity and the wisdom of the universe.

This card serves as a reminder that in some ancient rituals, women played the most important priestly roles. In these cults, the priestesses were consecrated to the goddess Diana, the goddess of the moon. Even today, moon-worshipping cults exist, but they operate clandestinely and under conditions of mystery.

In certain cases, this is the most important card in the Major Arcana.

In a spread

The significance of the "High Priestess" card in a spread lies in its secrecy, mystery, and enigma — all of which have to be hidden from the light of day and revealed only by the dim light of the moon. The card represents situations in which things must be hidden and not mentioned. Sometimes this card indicates some kind of mystical knowledge. It represents the feminine side, and complements the Magician.

If the card appears **upright**, it symbolizes secrets, wisdom, knowledge, vague future, and as yet unrevealed profound awareness. It can mean that the answers cannot be found. Your future is full of mystery. Your persistence and intelligence will play an important role in the future. It admonishes you not to waste words — remember that silence is golden.

If the card appears **in reverse**, it indicates either physical or spiritual desire, emotional instability and dark secrets. If you are a woman, the card hints at reproductive problems. If you are a man, it points at an unclear sexual identity. The card warns you to watch out for the dangers of vanity and superficiality. You will be exposed to extreme emotions.

Other important symbols contained in "The High Priestess" card:

1. The **diadem** on the Priestess' head and the **crescent moon** at her feet represent knowledge of the occult and the medium's skill.
2. **Wearing scarves** implies that more is concealed than is revealed, and this enhances the secretive atmosphere.
3. The **word TORA** engraved upside-down on the scroll held by the Priestess contributes to the feeling of strangeness, the unknown, and a lack of clarity.
4. The **symbols of the Torah, the cross, and the crescent** hint that true mystical knowledge knows no boundaries, and embraces all religions.
5. The **columns** represent Solomon's Pillars, named Boaz and Jachin, upon which Solomon built the Temple. The colors of the columns (black and white) represent masculine and feminine forces, and they also hint at the divine wisdom deep inside the Priestess.

An excess of color   A lack of color

The Empress 3

The main idea expressed in this card is that of plenty, fertility, luck, happiness and prosperity.

Description

The Empress reclines on a luxurious throne, dressed in a robe richly decorated with jewels and pomegranates. On her head is a triangular crown consisting of twelve stars, and in her right hand she holds a scepter adorned with a miniature orb of the Earth. Leaning against the throne on her right is a shield with the symbol of Venus on it. In the foreground, wheat grows abundantly, symbolizing the plenty that is associated with this card. Behind the Empress a stream flows among the trees of a forest, culminating in a waterfall. Every image in this card radiates a feeling of well-being and abundance.

The Empress is Heaven on Earth, an earthly Garden of Eden; she symbolizes the material human world. However, her status is above that of a mere human queen. She still holds the lofty position of the mother of all men, the queen of Nature, total femininity. She is the goddess of Earth, but is not a divine figure. Although she is the mother of all men and the symbol of the cycle of life, she is still above earthly things.

This card symbolizes the gate to the Garden of Venus, through which we enter the world. The High Priestess guards the secret of the path beyond the gate, so the Empress plays the role of intermediary between the querent and the High Priestess. But the Empress is the gateway.

The Empress is associated with the Greek goddess, Demeter, the goddess of the harvest, abundance and fertility, or the Middle Eastern Astarte, the fertility goddess.

In a spread

When the "Empress" card occurs in a spread, it is a wonderful sign of happiness, luck, prosperity, success, abundance and fertility. It promises the querent that his dreams will come true — and even more than that. Not only will the querent succeed in the realm in question — he will flourish in everything concerning him, in the broadest sense. For example, he will succeed both in a specific deal and generally in all financial matters.

If the card appears **upright**, it symbolizes social activity, sex, pregnancy, birth, motherhood, family, success, and economic prosperity. There are also some negative aspects, such as rudeness, distrust, mystery, and doubt. You will be required to display initiative and resourcefulness in the future. You may have to cope with uncertainty and a lack of knowledge.

If the card appears **in reverse**, it means publicity, revealing secrets, alienation of children, feminine problems, and sexual perversion. However, the reverse position also has a positive meaning: you will solve complicated issues, and this will help you reveal the truth and gain enlightenment. It may be difficult for you to reach a decision in the future.

Other important symbols contained in "The Empress" Card:

1. The **dress decorated with pomegranates**, the **wheat**, the **scepter made of a corn cob**, the **streams**, the **verdant vegetation**, and the **color of the** sky are all symbols of abundance and fertility.
2. The **number** of the card, 3, is considered a lucky number.
3. The **shape of the shield** and the **sign of Venus** are associated with love and beauty.
4. The **dozen stars comprising her crown** represent the months of the year and the Wheel of Fortune, and are symbols of absolute control over all the areas of life.
5. The **curves of the throne** signify lightness and harmony.

An excess of color   A lack of color

21

The Emperor   4

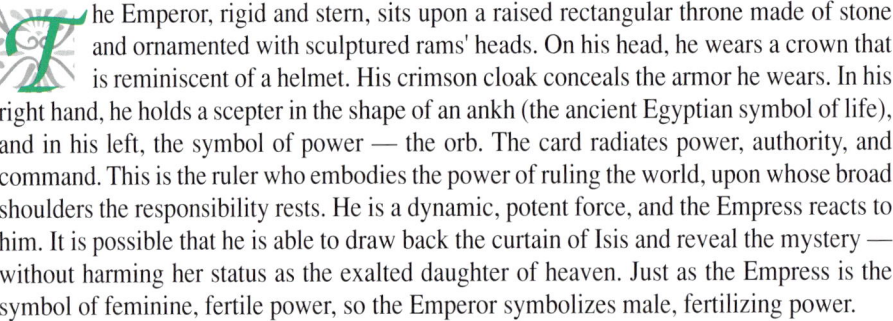

The main idea expressed in this card is that of

the power of the ruler.

Description

he Emperor, rigid and stern, sits upon a raised rectangular throne made of stone and ornamented with sculptured rams' heads. On his head, he wears a crown that is reminiscent of a helmet. His crimson cloak conceals the armor he wears. In his right hand, he holds a scepter in the shape of an ankh (the ancient Egyptian symbol of life), and in his left, the symbol of power — the orb. The card radiates power, authority, and command. This is the ruler who embodies the power of ruling the world, upon whose broad shoulders the responsibility rests. He is a dynamic, potent force, and the Empress reacts to him. It is possible that he is able to draw back the curtain of Isis and reveal the mystery — without harming her status as the exalted daughter of heaven. Just as the Empress is the symbol of feminine, fertile power, so the Emperor symbolizes male, fertilizing power.

Although it is not an overt fact that the Empress and Emperor are married, the relationship is implied. Certainly, they are united in their status of rulers; more significantly, however, they represent and control the spiritual throne of the Kingdom of Heaven — as well as the material, earthly one. Although the Emperor is sometimes interpreted as representing the power of the will, he is not linked with the absolute or the eternal.

The Emperor is identified with the Greek father of all gods, Zeus, who determined good and evil in the world, and gave laws and values to humanity. He conducted himself with mercy and compassion, but punished transgressors severely.

"The Emperor" is a controlling, authoritative card, representing the patriarch — the primary power.

In a spread

When "The Emperor" card occurs in a female querent's spread, it represents the principal masculine figure in her life — generally speaking, her husband. In exceptional cases, it represents her father. When the "Emperor" card occurs in a male querent's spread, it represents his father, and occasionally his boss. If there are no additional clues, the "Emperor" card represents success as a natural consequence of a position of power.

If the card appears **upright**, it signifies power, authority, stability, protection, aid, greatness, strong will, courage, the pinnacle, as well as the shouldering of responsibility. The card indicates that in the future, you will enjoy a solid basis and high standing. Furthermore, you can feel free from threat and danger.

If the card appears **in reverse**, it represents manipulative and critical behavior and difficulty with delegating authority; it exerts pressure and causes confusion. If you are a woman, it means that you have difficulties with your husband — possibly to the point of violence. If you are a man, it means that you are cowardly, seeking refuge behind a woman's skirt. The card encourages you to behave with kindness and empathy, and admonishes you that it is time for you to stop behaving childishly.

Other important symbols contained in "The Emperor" card:

1. The **helmet** and the **armor** hint at the power concealed under the Emperor's cloak; in other words, the power is not wielded hastily.
2. The **orb** and the **scepter** are obvious symbols of rule.
3. The **rams' heads** symbolize the power and daring required to lead the herd. This is also the astrological sign of Aries.
4. The **rectangular throne** and the **number of the card, 4**, symbolize the physical realm and the power of material things. In certain Tarot decks, the Emperor is depicted in a position reminiscent of the number 4.
5. The **precious stones** encrusting the helmet are a symbol of the wealth that derives from power.

An excess of color   A lack of color

23

The Hierophant 5

The main idea expressed in this card is

the establishment.

Description

The Hierophant is seated on his throne, and is preaching a sermon. He wears the papal miter (indeed, in old Tarot decks, he was sometimes called "The Pope," even though this image represents only some of his symbolism), and holds the papal triple cross in his left hand. His right hand forms the sign of the traditional Catholic blessing. He sits between two columns, but these are not the columns of the Temple (Boaz and Jachin) between which the High Priestess sits. While the High Priestess controls mystical, covert religion, the Hierophant is in charge of the external trappings and rituals of religion. The card exudes an atmosphere of religion and tradition, which is not surprising, since it originated during a time when the Church wielded prodigious power over everything: religion, government, justice, and everyday life.

In the foreground, two clerics listen to the Hierophant's sermon and bow to him. At his feet is a pair of crossed keys — a powerful symbol to some people, since they open the gates of wisdom, just as St. Peter holds the keys to Heaven.

The Hierophant represents what is holy and right in the physical world, and serves as the intermediary between the official world of the establishment and ordinary people. He is responsible for man's spiritual and religious salvation. However, although the Hierophant heads the theological order of the world, he is not the unequaled, absolute, divine authority, nor is he the essence of everything.

The Hierophant is connected to the figure of the pope, as we mentioned above. In order to avoid conflict with the church, however, the word "Pope" was changed to "Hierophant," which was the name of the high priest in the arcane ceremonies of ancient Athens and ancient Egypt. The pope, as the representative of Christ, symbolizes the living spirit of God in mortals, and this symbol is connected with a Greek god who sacrificed immortality in order to live as a mortal. During his life among human beings, he instilled spiritual values into them.

In a spread

In a spread, this card represents the institutions of law (the courts), of religion (the priesthood), of education (universities), and the establishment itself (municipal and federal offices). The Hierophant operates in the spiritual realm, and this card represents morality — both from the point of view of family and of religion.

If the card appears **upright**, it symbolizes religious service, marriage, divorce, law, religious matters and joys, conservatism, spiritual enlightenment, mercy and compassion. You will have a chance to display your innate compassion and good nature. You can expect to form some kind of relationship, such as marriage or a partnership, in the future. There is also a possibility of captivity.

If the card appears **in reverse**, it indicates avarice, mourning, hypocrisy, sexual crimes, weakness, obsequiousness, breakdown of the family, and bad advice. However, your astuteness will stand you in good stead in days to come. Don't let people take advantage of your good nature — it will make you appear weak.

Other important symbols contained in "The Hierophant" card:

1. The **miter** and the **cross** represent the institution of religion, as well as the establishment in general.
2. The **keys** are the heavenly keys of St. Peter, with which he opens the doors to the upper realms.
3. The **monks** emphasize the ceremonial significance of the event: without an audience, there are no ceremonies.
4. The **letter "W"** in the Hierophant's miter immortalizes the name of Waite, the creator of the deck.

An excess of color   A lack of color

The Lovers 6

The main idea expressed in this card is

the conflict between reason and emotion.

Description

Adam and Eve stand naked in the Garden of Eden, flanked by the Tree of Knowledge (near Eve), which possesses the knowledge of good and evil, and the Tree of Life (near Adam). The sun shines in the sky above them, and a benevolent, protective, winged figure, symbolizing the Divine Spirit, separates man from heaven and acts as his intermediary. While the two figures represent the innocent, pure, and platonic love that existed before they ate the fruit of the Tree of Knowledge, temptation and seduction are personified by the snake curled around the trunk.

The card, which is the first in the Major Arcana to contain two central human figures, symbolizes human love, not just marriage. It is sometimes interpreted on the level of black magic. The role of the woman is to enable man's nature to become complete, thus allowing him to rise to a higher plane. With her mystery, she draws him to the law of Divine Providence as well as to an emotional life.

The card embodies the conflict between emotion and reason, heart and mind, intuition and cold logic. The card is reminiscent of the Greek myth about a foolish man called Paris, who was awarded the world's most beautiful woman, Helen of Troy, to marry. However, she was already married. This incident resulted in the Trojan War.

In a spread

In a spread, this card represents a serious dilemma, a conflict between two choices, one based on reason and logical considerations, and the other on emotion and desires: good and evil, Heaven (God) or Hell (the Devil). Although there is an element of sexual desire and temptation, the card, despite its name, does not necessarily deal with romantic love. Its main thrust is in the direction of the choice based on logic and reason.

If the card appears **upright**, it means beauty, love, attraction, and surmounting obstacles. If you are a man, the card represents a challenge; if you are a woman, it represents a struggle. It also hints that you may experiences love problems concerned with choices. However, you will triumph over the obstacles in your path. Love and passion await you in the future.

If the card appears **in reverse**, it indicates setbacks and frustrations in love, even a loss of libido. It also means conjugal problems. For a man, it may represent impotence; for a woman — not realizing her full sexual potential. The card warns that if you don't act cautiously, you will not succeed in either your plans or your relationship.

Other important symbols contained in "The Lovers" card:

1. The **Divine Spirit** symbolizes morality, reason, and the superego.
2. The **snake** represents the emotional side, lust, and the id.
3. The **Tree of Life** represents immortality with its twelve fruits — a symbol of an infinite cycle.
4. The **Tree of Knowledge** bears four fruits — a number that symbolizes the material world and teaches that knowledge simultaneously liberates and imprisons.
5. The fact that **Adam looks at Eve while Eve looks at God** symbolizes confusion and the fact that their outlooks do not coincide.

An excess of color   A lack of color

27

The Chariot 7

The main idea expressed in this card is

that although the querent's situation is stable and sure, he or she is not in control.

Description

A regal figure, dressed in festive garments and holding a spear in his right hand, stands steadfastly in a canopied chariot. His stance symbolizes security and safety. On his shoulders are the *Urim and Thummim*, the symbols of the oracle of the High Priest in the Temple; he also wears the priestly tunic and breastplate. He is moving toward victory, progress, and success — intellectual and scientific. However, his forward movement does not depend on his hands, as the sphinxes that are supposed to be pulling his chariot are not harnessed to it, and he is not holding any reins. The *Urim and Thummim*, as well as the white and black opposites, mean that any forward movement depends entirely on the figure's power of reason and logic. In the background stand the city and its ramparts, but these are extraneous to the figure.

The sphinxes are symbols of mystery that the figure has to face and decipher. He does this by means of his mental powers. They represent nature's enigmas — cold and heat, night and day. One sphinx is black and one is white, which is reminiscent of the "Boaz" and "Jachin" columns in the Temple of the High Priestess. The chariot, however, cannot pass through the columns into the Temple, nor can the Torah scroll save the figure. He cannot answer the Priestess' riddles. His status is anomalous vis-à-vis the six preceding cards. This card constitutes a bridge between the first septet of Tarot cards (which concentrate on the ethereal and the spiritual) and the second (which is more earthly and physical).

There is a link to the biblical figure of Joseph in this card: the chariot — a gift from Pharaoh; the number 7, symbolizing the seven sheaves, the seven good years and the seven bad years; the sphinxes, an Egyptian symbol, representing Joseph's service in Pharaoh's court. The lack of control symbolized by this card reflects the fact that Joseph, as a foreigner, did not possess genuine power.

In a spread

In a spread, this card represents comfort and stability, without control. The querent's status may be secure, but he is neither pulling the strings nor calling the moves.

If the card appears **upright**, it means possible advancement in life, victory (in war, too), vengeance, ambition, hesitation, problems and conquering fears. You will be helped in the future — possibly by a more powerful force than your fellow human beings. Be careful not to fall into the trap of seeking revenge.

If the card appears **in reverse**, it signifies conflicts, defeat, mishaps, possible mental illness, and mobility problems — either in travel or up the ladder of advancement. You are warned about serious conflicts — even physical battles — and bitter defeats.

Other important symbols contained in "The Chariot" card:

1. The **four poles** symbolize material temptations (the number 4 represents the material world).
2. The **sky-blue, star-adorned canopy** symbolizes Joseph's triumph over material temptations.
3. The **red symbol** on the front of the chariot was originally a graphic representation of the male member penetrating the female organ — symbolizing Potiphar's wife's unsuccessful attempt to seduce Joseph.
4. The **blue wings** represent the triumph of the spirit over the material.

An excess of color   A lack of color

Strength 8

The main idea expressed in this card is

that every cloud has a silver lining.

Description

This is the first card in the Major Arcana to describe a quality rather than a particular figure. The quality is personified by a young woman, whose hair and dress are adorned with flowers, and above whose head floats the symbol of infinity (the Divine) — as in "The Fool" card. She is closing the jaws of a lion gently, fearlessly, calmly, and firmly. She is the symbol of strength that derives from total belief in and acceptance of divine law, which protects, strengthens, and supports her. As a result, she exercises total control over the most powerful of creatures.

The lion is already tame; this is symbolized by the fact that he is wearing a wreath of flowers around his neck, as well as by his tongue, which is licking the woman's arm. The wreath also signifies the burden of divine law, which is easy to bear when the person's faith is genuine and heartfelt.

The strength illustrated in this card is an ethereal, spiritual strength rather than simply a physical one. Although the woman's demeanor expresses self-confidence, it is not mere bravado; it is her deep-rooted faith in the Almighty, as well as her ability to conquer her desires, thus bolstering her personal fortitude, which enables her to deal with the lion as if he were a harmless cub.

The card derives from two mythological sources. The first is the story of Samson, who broke the lion's jaw. Afterwards, bees nested in the dead lion, and produced honey. The second is a Greek myth about a maiden who fought with a lion and killed it. The god Apollo was so impressed that he granted her eternal life.

In a spread

In a spread, the card describes situations of daring behavior leading to rewards (like the honey pouring out of the dead lion's jaws). It represents achievements and happiness brought about by a certain degree of aggressiveness and audacity. An additional meaning is that of the "silver lining": even if everything seems to be lost in a certain situation, it might ultimately become a triumph.

If the card appears **upright**, it represents courage, action, strength, energy, health, the accomplishment of objectives, achievements, the conquest of bodily desires, and spiritual strength that leads to clairvoyant and healing powers. You will have the opportunity of displaying your positive attributes, such as your ability to take action and to work energetically. You will be successful in the future.

If the card appears **in reverse**, it symbolizes the power to corrupt, tyranny, weakness, illness, sexual perversion, self-hatred, and physical misdemeanors. It warns you not to let power go to your head; if you abuse it, you run the risk of a rapid downfall and shame.

Other important symbols in "The Strength" card:

1. The **flower-bedecked** maiden symbolizes gentleness and femininity.
2. The **lion** symbolizes power and masculinity.
3. The **symbol of infinity** indicates divine providence.

An excess of color   A lack of color

The Hermit 9

The main idea expressed in this card is

that of soul-searching.

Description

The tall figure of the hermit, wearing a hooded monk's robe, stands on the snowy peak of a mountain, one hand grasping a staff and the other holding a lantern (a symbol of antiquity) lit by a shining star (the light of the world). He is looking downward. The card radiates an atmosphere of contemplation and solitude, which is appropriate for the quest for truth and justice. To aid him in his quest are the staff, which symbolizes wandering and journeys, and the lantern, which lights the way. The fact that the hermit is looking downward may represent introspection, looking inside his own heart for truth and justice. The staff is as tall as the hermit is, perhaps signifying that his quest is long and difficult — even a lifelong one.

The idea of solitude on a mountain peak is ancient and widespread: Moses climbed Mount Sinai in search of enlightenment, and wise men throughout the ages — even today, in the Far East — have sought "divine wisdom and justice" by isolating themselves from the rest of humanity high up in the mountains, walking toward the dawn by the light of lanterns. According to the mystics, this is the only way to conduct a true soul-searching.

In a spread

In a spread, the card represents a kind of "time out," a time for the querent to separate himself from others and conduct a soul-searching, a personal reckoning. It represents a state of limbo, of suspended animation, while the querent deliberates, ponders, analyzes, and contemplates the inner questions that preoccupy him.

If the card appears **upright**, it symbolizes the positive attributes of peace, enlightenment, and wisdom. It has, however, some negative attributes, which are corruption and apathy. It influences the other cards in the spread and points the way. You must act cautiously and tactfully in the future. Watch out for other people's betrayal and two-faced conduct.

If the card appears **in reverse**, it represents fear, alienation, a lack of logic, and taking the wrong path in life. If you do not act in a straightforward manner, you will be haunted by anxiety. Don't hide behind false appearances.

Other important symbols contained in "The Hermit" card:
1. The **staff** is a symbol of the wanderer, while the **lamp** is an indication of the quest for truth.
2. The **asceticism and plainness** of the card means that the truth is inside the person, and does not depend on external trappings.
3. The **dark sky** hints at the gloom of solitude.
4. The **snowy mountain peak** reminds us that we can only discover our mistakes by looking at them from above.

An excess of color  A lack of color

33

Wheel of Fortune   10

The number of this card in Tarot is 10
(which has a numerological significance).
The main idea expressed in this card is
the vagaries of fate, as well as the natural ups and downs of life.

Description

This complex card embodies the mysticism and esoteric symbols of the Tarot philosophy. There is no central human image here: the Wheel of Fortune (or Fate) is the protagonist, with its concentric circles and perpetual motion.

The inner band of the wheel consists of the alchemical symbols (salt, water, mercury and sulfur) of the four elements (earth, water, air and fire). The outer one comprises the four mystical Hebrew letters that form the Tetragrammaton, the unpronounceable name of God — ה ו ה י — and the four Latin letters that form three words: TORA (Torah – see the High Priestess), ROTA (Latin for "wheel") or TARO (Tarot). Along the wheel's outer edge are three Egyptian symbols: the sword-brandishing Sphinx, balancing the movement of the wheel, Typhon the snake, and Anubis, god of the dead, half jackal and half human. The wheel illustrates the idea of stability that is effected by perfectly balanced motion (like a gyroscope).

Shrouded in clouds in the four corners of the card are the four Kabbalistic symbols of angels (cherubim): man (symbolizing air), eagle (water), lion (fire), and bull (earth) — which comprise the vision of Ezekiel or of St. John. They are all reading books.

The number 4 features prominently in this card: the Tetragrammaton, the four elements, their four alchemical symbols, the four cherubim, as well as the cyclical nature of the number four (the ancient Chinese law of cyclical flow, seen in the endless cycles of seasons or weeks of the month). Only the Egyptian symbols are three. The two numbers, 3 and 4, represent the whole Tarot system.

In old Tarot cards, the Wheel of Fortune depicted the blindfolded goddess Fortuna spinning the wheel, and figures trying to climb up the wheel or falling off. This served to illustrate the vagaries of fate, the ups and downs of life, and the inevitability of birth, maturity, decline, and death.

In a spread

In a spread, the card represents a period of upheaval and change, for better or for worse, from the heights of joy to the depths of despair, over which the querent has no control: he is in the hands of Fate, which may not necessarily be bad.

If the card appears **upright**, it represents good fortune, success, fate, a successful gamble, a positive move, a pleasant surprise, and control over your life. The future holds a lot of good fortune and happiness for you. You can expect a rise in status.

If the card appears in **reverse**, it means a reverse of fortune, instability, succumbing to the whims of fate, and a lack of confidence. It can sometimes mean apathy and death, if the wheel's motion ceases. You can look forward to a life of plenty — just be careful that you don't become wasteful.

Other important symbols contained in "The Wheel of Fortune" card:

1. The **wheel** symbolizes cycles, rising and falling, changes, while **the four signs of the Zodiac** below represent the infinite cyclical nature of the seasons.
2. The **lion** represents the sign of the Zodiac, Aries, the element of fire.
3. The **angel** represents the sign of the Zodiac, Aquarius, the element of air.
4. The **bull** represents the sign of the Zodiac, Taurus, the element of earth.
5. The **eagle** represents the sign of the Zodiac, Scorpio, the element of water.

An excess of color   A lack of color

Justice 11

The main idea expressed in this card is

that your past deeds catch up with your in the present.

Description

The stern goddess of Justice, wearing the crown of authority on her head and a crimson robe, is seated on the throne of justice between two columns (good and evil) with a curtain draped between them. These symbolize the moral principles according to which every person chooses to lead his life, especially that of free choice. Justice holds the sword of wisdom in her right hand, ready to punish anyone who fails the test of the scales (held in her left hand) if his bad deeds outweigh his good ones. The symbols in this card are basically negative ones, as there is no reward, only punishment. By making the correct choice (of good), man can elevate himself. There are neither alternatives nor compromises in justice.

While this card is reminiscent of the High Priestess, who sits between the Temple columns and personifies mystical and arcane wisdom, Justice sits on the threshold of quite another world.

The mythological sources of this card lie in ancient Greece and ancient Egypt, both of which had goddesses who represented Justice and who meted out penalties to those whose good deeds were found wanting. In both cases, there was punishment for offenders, but no reward for those who passed the test of the scales. The goddess of Justice punishes only those people who are responsible for their evil actions, not those who were the victims of fate or circumstances.

In a spread

In a spread, the main meaning of the card is that one's deeds catch up with one sooner or later. The symbol of the scales hints at legal proceedings as a result of divorce, dismissal from a job, financial losses, and so on — something for which the querent is totally responsible. One of the following cards will often occur with the card of Justice: King of Swords, Prince of Wands, or The Hierophant.

If the card appears **upright**, it represents reward and punishment, honesty, sincerity, the triumph of justice, and the acknowledgment of social norms. Your talents for balanced judgment will come to the fore in the future. If you are involved in legal proceedings, your honesty will prevail, and you will win the case.

If the card appears **in reverse**, it means guilt feelings, hypocrisy, two-faced behavior, coercion, a lack of balance, and law. Watch out for the long arm of the law — it can embroil you in complications you never dreamed of. Be warned of losses and exaggerated consequences.

Other important symbols contained in "The Justice" card:
1. The **crimson robe** emphasizes the quality of justice that the goddess embodies.
2. The **sword** symbolizes justice and the severity of the punishment.
3. The **curtain** symbolizes the divide between the revealed and the concealed, telling us that our overt deeds are judged covertly, with no possibility of advocacy.

An excess of color  A lack of color

37

The Hanged Man 12

The main idea expressed in this card is

sacrifice and the victory of the spirit over matter.

Description

A man is suspended upside-down from a Tau cross. His right foot is bound to the junction of the two axes of the cross, while his left leg forms another cross by bending under his right leg. Although it would be logical to assume that this is one of the ultimate forms of suffering, the man's face expresses serenity, even radiance, as is reflected in the glowing halo surrounding his head. The fact that he forms a cross with his own body testifies to holiness through sacrifice. Some people might call the man a martyr, calm even in the face of torture because of his unswerving belief in his ideals.

This cross was used by the Romans as an instrument of execution. Reverse crucifixion, that is, being suspended by the feet, was an added element of humiliation. In contrast to the agony and death symbolized by the cross, however, fresh leaves grow out of it, signifying that life still goes on. The leaves and the man's serene expression together create a sense of life rather than of wretched death.

This card can be seen as symbolizing the realm between Heaven and Earth, between the celestial and the terrestrial — a kind of limbo in which the Hanged Man finds himself, having sacrificed the physical and material, but not quite having achieved the divine, although he is well on the way. The card can be seen as representing resurrection — a renewal of life after death.

The concept of sacrifice exists in many religions: Abraham was willing to sacrifice Isaac to prove his devotion to God, Jesus forfeited his life for the redemption of humanity, Buddha gave up happiness and comfort in order to achieve enlightenment. The message is that nothing is given for nothing.

In a spread

In a spread, this card indicates that sacrifices must be made in order to obtain something better. Sometimes, however, sacrifice is inevitable and involuntary, simply because a person cannot hold on to something, and is compelled to give it up. Thus, there is also an element of compromise. This card means the triumph of the spiritual over the material.

If the card appears **upright**, it signifies prophetic ability, intuition, wisdom, self-sacrifice, setting an example, and sacrificing something in the present in favor of something else in the future. You must concentrate on your powers of prediction and soothsaying. In the future, you will be called upon to display your wisdom.

If the card appears **in reverse**, it indicates a "herd" mentality, egoism, punishment for transgressions, masochism, hypocrisy in politics, and the humiliation of others. The card warns you not to succumb to egoistic inclinations. You must take care not to be swept along by the opinion of the majority.

Other important symbols contained in "The Hanged Man" card:

1. The **hanged man** is a symbol of self-sacrifice in order to attain something of greater value.
2. The **halo** is a symbol of a whole-hearted sacrifice, meaning that the victim feels no bitterness, only elation.
3. The man's **crossed legs** are reminiscent of the shape of the cross.

An excess of color    A lack of color

Death

13

The number of this card in Tarot is 13 — a number that is considered good or bad, depending on the particular culture.

The main idea expressed in this card is

renewal, the end of one cycle (death) and the beginning of another (birth).

Description

An armor-clad skeleton, holding a black flag adorned with a white rose, rides a white horse slowly through a field, crushing the creatures and plants in his path. A man lies on his back, dead in the mud. His crown is under the horse's hoof. Three figures stand in front of him: a little girl, staring in wonder at the fearsome rider, a kneeling young girl, who is so overwhelmed by the sight that she is on the verge of fainting, and an elderly male figure, a bishop wearing his robes and miter, supplicating with the skeleton, who does not even look at him. The card depicts the cycle of life: childhood, adolescence, maturity, and old age.

In the background, a river flows, and the sun rises between two tower-like structures, symbolizing eternity. The rose is a symbol of life, and as such is a spiritual symbol. The power of the rider lies in his ability to make even the most powerful people surrender, even though he carries no weapon. Death in this card is physical, natural, and inevitable, unlike the spiritual death and implied resurrection of the Hanged Man. However, man considers Death something mystical and mysterious, something that lurks behind towers, in unknown realms. As a result, the card is interpreted by occultists as rebirth and renewal rather than physical death.

Death appears throughout cultures and religions as the Black Prince, as the Angel of Death, on horseback, with a flaming sword. Mystics prefer to think of death as a stage in the eternal cycle of life, death, and rebirth rather than as something final.

In a spread

In a spread, the card is an indication of situations in which a person terminates his previous business or affairs and begins something completely new and different. It is not considered to be a good card, whether upright or in reverse.

If the card appears **upright**, it symbolizes destruction, termination, corruption, failed marriage, and losing a position of strength. You must watch out for your interests; there are people who seek your downfall and ruin. If you are a woman, you will have to deal with many problems. If you are an unmarried woman, you may suffer a disappointment in love.

If the card appears in **reverse**, all the above are magnified, in addition to difficulties, despair, and death. You will have to face the challenge of inactivity and apathy. There may be a disappointment in the future.

Other important symbols contained in "The Death" card:

1. The **black prince on his white horse** represents renewal through destruction.
2. The **human figures** symbolize the omnipotence of death, which spares no one, regardless of rank and status.
3. The **rising sun** is a symbol of divine light.
4. The **little girl**, staring at the horseman in wonder, symbolizes the ability of the very young to accept change.
5. The **rose** is a symbol of mystical groups.

An excess of color    A lack of color

Temperance — 14

The main idea expressed in this card is

holding the stick at both ends, merging different things.

Description

An asexual angel with outspread wings stands with one foot in a pool of water and the other on a rock (the symbol of nature), pouring the essence of life from a goblet held in its left hand into a goblet held in its right, without spilling a drop. The angle of pouring is impossible in reality. This is the meaning of the card: success at something that seems impossible, that is, holding the stick at both ends.

On the angel's forehead, there is a shining sun symbol, which might also signify the "third eye" — divine enlightenment, or the third part of the Trinity. On the angel's breast, there is a square containing a triangle, the sign of perfect balance. The triangle represents the Major Arcana, with seven cards on each side (excluding the Fool, which stands alone). The square represents the Minor Arcana, with 14 cards on each side. In other words, these are the Tarot symbols. Above the square appears the Tetragrammaton, the unpronounceable name of God — י ה ו ה, which represents the movement from stage to stage in the Major Arcana.

In the background, on the left, a long path leads to the summit of a mountain, above which the sun rises in a glorious blaze, indicating that man can achieve excellence and spiritual illumination, but the path is long and arduous. To the right, there is a clump of irises, indicating the cyclical nature of the seasons. The card contains symbols of the merging of male and female, the combination of ideas. When the concept of Temperance is achieved, the components of human nature unify into a harmonious whole, combining the spiritual and the physical. The person then has logical insight into the meaning of life.

This card has roots in the story of King David, who felt thirsty during a battle with the Philistines. Three of his men broke through enemy lines to find water for their king. This is the essence of the card: accomplishing the impossible in the face of all odds. Another interpretation, that of merging, originates from alchemy: attempts were made to combine two incompatible metals, gold and silver, in order to create a new, positive element.

In a spread

In a spread, this card signifies that the querent has succeeded in doing what is ostensibly impossible.

If the card appears **upright**, it represents moderation, compromise, prosperity, patience, and a talent for management, science, and the arts. You will have the chance to show your ability to save money and live frugally in the future. Your management abilities will come to the fore.

If the card appears **in reverse**, it is an indication of haplessness, difficulties, blind religiosity, erratic moods, possible schizophrenia, hypocrisy, and antagonism. You will be exposed to things concerning religion and religious functionaries. Watch out for conflicts of interests.

Other important symbols contained in "The Temperance" card:

1. The **two goblets** symbolize different forces that the angel links together.
2. The **sun rising between two peaks** is also a symbol of different forces that are linked together.
3. The **irises** symbolize the Greek goddess, Iris.
4. The **circle enclosing a dot** on the angel's forehead is the astrological symbol of the sun.

An excess of color    A lack of color

The Devil   15

The main idea expressed in this card is

corrupt impulses, the struggle between darkness and light.

Description

The beast-like Devil, with his piercing gaze, curved ram's horns, bat's wings, clawed feet, and hairy legs and genital region, crouches on an altar, his right hand raised in a diabolical salute. On his head, between the horns, is an inverted pentagram, indicating that the five senses are absent here. His whole demeanor exudes sexual depravity and bestiality. His left hand holds a burning torch downward, toward the fires of Hell. The background is entirely black, symbolizing night and the absence of divine illumination.

In front of him, loosely chained by the neck to a metal loop attached to the altar, are two naked figures: a female and a male, both with horns and tails. They are reminiscent of Adam and Eve after their expulsion from the Garden of Eden. The chains represent the material bonds that the figures are at liberty to remove, since their hands are not bound. However, they do not look as if they are suffering. The woman voluptuously plucks grapes from the bunch at the end of her tail. The faces of the two figures reveal human wisdom that tells them that they can be liberated from the Devil's dominance — but only by divine providence.

This card symbolizes the evil that people voluntarily choose to do. Unlike the Death card, which represents the inexorable and inevitable nature of the life cycle, the card of the Devil embodies evil and depravity. In Judaism, the Devil appears in the guise of the seductive snake; in Christianity, as the antichrist brandishing an inverted cross; and in Greek mythology, as the god Pan who is characterized by sexual excesses and perversions.

In a spread

In a spread, the card represents darkness, corruption, lechery, and base instincts; it must be seen as having diabolical energy. Its appearance warns of temptations, spurious deals, wickedness, and so on. If the High Priestess also appears, it is a sign that someone is using black magic to undermine the querent.

If the card appears **upright**, it symbolizes violence, lechery, overt sexuality, energy, pride, domestic problems, hedonism, physical weakness, leadership, and excessive, therefore destructive, charisma. Be on the lookout for damage and violence in the future. You will display your abilities to make superhuman efforts and be extremely emphatic. You cannot fight your fate — but this can be a good thing.

If it appears **in reverse**, it indicates spiritual blindness, sexual depravity, weakness, an attraction to crime, and evil influence. Whatever is bad when the card is upright is horrendous when it is in reverse. Be careful of petty, nit-picking behavior in the future. You may encounter a situation in which you have to force yourself to be strong.

Other important symbols contained in "The Devil" card:
1. The **devil's appearance** symbolizes depravity and debauchery.
2. The **inverted torc**h represents the inverted cross, which is used in black magic rituals.
3. The **square stone** upon which the Devil is seated symbolizes the material world (because of its four sides).
4. The **chains** represent the bonds of the material world.
5. The **bat's wings** and **dark background** symbolize the forces of darkness.

An excess of color   A lack of color

The Tower   16

The main idea expressed in this card is

destruction, the collapse of the existing, and the futility and transience of the material world when it has no spiritual base.

Description

A bolt of lightning strikes a tall tower standing on a bare cliff, igniting it and sending its dome flying. Flames belch out of the exposed top, as well as from the windows. Two terrified figures, one crowned, plummet down into the abyss. The various images of destruction mentioned above indicate that they do not have much hope of survival. The structure, also known as "The Lightning-Struck Tower" or "The Tower of Babel," is about to collapse — symbolizing destruction in any area. Some people claim that this card symbolizes the fall of man — the expulsion from the Garden of Eden — which explains the fall from light into darkness. Another explanation is the fact that the spiritual world is falling victim to materialism, meaning that thought, or free spirit, which aims to reveal God's mysteries, is dying.

Each figure is accompanied by individual flames — 10 on the side of the crowned figure, and 12 on the other side. The total, 22, represents the number of cards in the Major Arcana, the number of letters in the Hebrew alphabet, or the parts of the Kabbalistic Tree of Life. Their only hope lies in the 12 signs of the Zodiac or the 10 spheres of the Tree of Life.

The mystical roots of this card originate in the story of the Tower of Babel, in which God caused everyone involved in its construction to speak a different language. According to the mystics, in order to understand the mysteries of the universe, a special language is required, and God did not want humanity to learn it. Thus, he gave each person a different language. A mystic has to undergo a process of destroying all of his knowledge and values, then rebuilding them in order to acquire the tools for understanding creation. This card, unlike the renewal and cyclical Death card, represents only destruction and collapse.

In a spread

In a spread, the Tower card represents the collapse or destruction of whatever the preceding card in the spread indicated. This can be good or bad, depending on the card.

If the card appears **upright**, it indicates destruction, disintegration, suffering, depression, crumbling relationships, financial insecurity, accidents, disease, and collapsing frameworks. You will have to take great care in the future if you want to avoid the unexpected calamities and hardships this card represents. There is the danger of betrayal by people around you, leading to ruin and disgrace.

If the card appears **in reverse**, it is better than upright, as it gives warning of all the characteristics of the upright card, as well as of impending danger. You can expect similar, if slightly less serious, events. Be very aware of what's going on around you — other people's actions can be tyrannical, and even lead to incarceration.

Other important symbols contained in "The Tower" card:

1. The **tower** is a symbol of the material world, where even the strongest objects can be shattered in an instant by a blow of fate.
2. The **lightning** symbolizes a phenomenon that takes place instantaneously, and is not a lengthy process.
3. The **crown** represents the mortality and vulnerability of all people — even kings.

An excess of color   A lack of color

The Star   17

The main idea expressed in this card is

cautious optimism and possible change for the better.

Description

The card depicts a naked maiden kneeling at the edge of a lake, one foot in the water, the other on the ground, symbolizing the unity of opposites. She is pouring two jugs of the water of life — one into the lake, the other onto the earth. Behind her, on a tree at the top of a hill, sits a bird with outstretched wings, as if preparing for flight. This is significant, as it symbolizes man's ability to rise up toward divine light by means of the pure truth.

Above her is a large, eight-pointed star, surrounded by seven smaller eight-pointed stars (representing the planets that were known at the time). The central star, with the help of its eight auxiliaries, illuminates the card instead of the sun.

The card radiates an atmosphere of beauty and innocence, of purity and hope. The maiden represents youth and beauty (spiritual rather than physical), and her nakedness symbolizes innocence and the pure, naked truth. All of these elements join together in the maiden as an acknowledgment of the greatness of the heavens. This card is sometimes referred to as "The Well of the Waters of Life" or "The Gifts of the Spirit."

The main message of this card is hope; the maiden, pure and innocent, gives the most precious gift: the water of life. She represents the aspect of divine understanding in the Kabbala, and for this reason she pours her wisdom onto inferior realms.

The card reminds us of the Fountain of Youth, or the Elixir of Life in alchemy. In addition, it implies that some of the bounty given to us by God should be returned to Him in order to receive His blessing — whence the idea of harvest festivals, sacrifices, tithes, and so on. Thus the maiden returns some of the water of life to its source, in gratitude for having been given so much.

In a spread

In a spread, the card signifies cautious optimism and a positive situation, which, however, is not yet signed and sealed: there is still something that the querent has to do in order to ensure success or victory. The card can indicate honest intentions, innocence, and a clear conscience.

If the card appears **upright**, it indicates new talents to be developed, hope for better things, and surmounting obstacles. It can also signify disease, danger, and setbacks. The future holds two possible directions for you — one is full of hope and opportunity, while the other contains negative things such as burglary, loss, and abandonment. Try to emphasize the positive direction.

If the card appears **in reverse**, it means disappointment, problems, illness, danger of death, impotence, and calls for help. You must refrain from overbearing and condescending behavior. Watch out for other people who want to render you powerless.

Other important symbols contained in "The Star" card:

1. The **maiden's nudity** symbolizes purity and having nothing to hide — properties that are mandatory for finding the spring of youth.
2. **Pouring water into water** is an ostensibly meaningless action, but it symbolizes anointing in magic rites to ensure abundance and fertility.
3. **Pouring water onto the earth** is a symbol of growth — as can be seen from the greening **field**.
4. The **eight-pointed star**, replacing the horizontal 8 of the symbol of infinity, symbolizes divine providence.
5. The **bird poised for flight** symbolizes potential power, and this strikes a discordant note in the idyllic, tranquil scene.

An excess of color   **A lack of color**

49

The Moon 18

The main idea expressed in this card is

feminine wisdom and nocturnal fantasy.

Description

The moon, which is a composite of a full moon with 32 rays beaming from it, a crescent, and a cold, unfriendly female profile, is rising above two towers, which closely resemble the ones in the Death card. Fifteen drops of dew, ice, or frost are either falling to the earth or being pulled up by lunar gravity to the moon. The moon seems to be covering the earth with coldness.

A dog and a wolf are baying at the moon; they represent man's fears of the unknown, especially in the dark, with only dim, reflected moonlight to guide him. This dull light emphasizes man's animal nature, also represented by the dog and the wolf. A crab is crawling out of the water in the foreground, in the direction of a path that begins at the water's edge and winds its way to the hills on the horizon. The path symbolizes the journey to the unknown, and links this world to the next world. The crab, which attempts to crawl out of the water, and then probably falls back again, also represents man's struggle to raise himself up. The moon's power of attraction can also be seen to be responsible for the tides, and for drawing the crab out of the water (the subconscious) onto the land (the familiar).

The card symbolizes the world of the imagination — of nightmares, fantasies, dreams, illusions, lunacy, or simply a rich imagination. It is connected with Hecate, the goddess of the dark side of the moon, whose symbols are the dog and the wolf, which guide the souls of the dead in the underworld. Death and sleep are interconnected, and, as the moon has always symbolized insanity, there is but a short step to lunacy.

In a spread

In a spread, this card signifies a difficult time: insomnia, nightmares, worries, etc. It expresses emotions, not actions. It can also indicate feverish creativity, but it needs other cards, such as King of Swords, etc., to be present in the spread. Sometimes it indicates a maternal figure, but this requires the King of Cups as well. It can also signify magical powers, but for this it needs the High Priestess or the Devil.

If the card appears **upright**, it means overcoming difficulties. It warns against danger, hidden enemies, mistakes, and a tendency toward mysticism. There are perils and treachery awaiting the hapless querent in the future. Be alert and fearless in order to counteract the forces of evil and darkness.

If the card appears **in reverse**, it is a very bad sign, as it indicates acute disease, instability, and a cry for help. It warns you to watch out for other people who want to undermine your stability through betrayal and misrepresentation. In the future, see that you avoid a lack of constancy.

Other important symbols contained in "The Moon" card:
1. The **dewdrops** and the **pond** symbolize the female element of water, as well as the moon's magnetic power.
2. The **crab** — Cancer in the Zodiac — is also a water sign, dominated by the moon.
3. The **profile** in the moon symbolizes the moon's multifarious nature.

An excess of color   A lack of color

The Sun 19

The main idea expressed in this card is

success that comes from the outside.

Description

In the foreground, a naked young child rides happily on a white horse. He holds a huge red banner in his left hand. Behind him is a garden wall, over which masses of large sunflowers peep. Above the sunflowers is a large, fully frontal, benevolent sun, representing the consciousness of the spirit in a direct and piercing way (as opposed to the secrecy and concealment of the moon's profile in the previous card, and its indirect, reflected light). Twenty-one visible straight and wavy rays emanate from the sun, representing the 21 cards in the Major Arcana, while a single hidden wavy ray, at the top, indicates the Fool.

This card radiates happiness, directness, and light, and symbolizes the hope for a better future. It hints at the passage of the obvious solar light on the earth to the unknown, hidden light of the next world, as symbolized by the innocent, guileless, naked child. These two forms of light will gradually unite as the child grows. The child also signifies the nucleus containing the essence of wisdom that will redeem and guard the world.

This card represents the masculine symbol of Apollo, the Greek sun god, who gives unstintingly without demanding anything in return. It is linked to the physical, material world, while the moon is involved with spirituality and mysticism. It is active and masculine, while the moon is passive and feminine.

In a spread

In a spread, the Sun represents great success in every field — with the assistance of outside factors.

If the card appears **upright**, it signifies happiness, conjugal bliss, prosperity, and a great deal of love, respect, and self-confidence. You will be prosperous and content in the future. The future holds a good marriage for you.

If the card appears **in reverse**, it foretells financial worries, problems, a difficult period ahead, dependency, and a big decrease in the meanings of an upright card in the spread. It also signifies a slightly lesser degree of the upright prediction.

Other important symbols in "The Sun" card:

1. The **banner-bearing child** symbolizes masculinity and fertilizing power, as does the **horse**.
2. The **sunflowers** symbolize the sun.
3. The **wall** represents not only protection, but the fact that wealth and happiness are limited to the material world, while spiritual bliss lies beyond its confines.

An excess of color   A lack of color

Judgement 20

The main idea expressed in this card is

enlightenment and sobriety, along with rebirth.

Description

On the face of it, this card depicts Judgement Day, when the dead rise from their graves to be judged. The angel, wreathed in clouds, blows a trumpet draped in a flag decorated with a cross. The trumpet symbolizes man's inner voice, striving to reach God, pulling his body with it. Recognizing the inner voice enables man to believe in eternal life.

Two families, one in the foreground with their backs to the viewer, and one in the background facing the viewer, stand up, lift their faces, and stretch out their hands in an ecstatic and supplicating manner toward the angel. Their joy derives from the hope of resurrection through prayer and divine intervention.

Symbolically, the card is an indication of awakening, dread, sobriety, and enlightenment. According to Christian tradition, the angel is St. Michael, who is linked with Mercury, the god who directs the souls in the underworld. Michael's job is to open people's eyes to the objective reality of the world, as happened to Abraham, Moses, Buddha, and Muhammed.

In a spread

In a spread, this card forces the querent to open his eyes and see reality as it is, with no embellishments or rose-colored glasses. This sudden unveiled revelation will be a turning point that leads the querent to make important decisions. The cards on either side of the Judgement card must be examined in order to know where the querent is coming from and where he is going.

If the card appears **upright**, it signifies rebirth, renewal, sexuality, a new status, reward for past actions, the end of a negative relationship, a successful beginning, and a new opportunity. You will get a new job in the future. It is good for you to begin a process of self-renewal. Watch out for an adverse ruling in a lawsuit.

If the card appears **in reverse**, it indicates a loss of prosperity leading to a lower status, disease, death, weakness, a non-start beginning, and purposelessness. Do not let cowardice and weakness ruin your chances in the future. Let your considered, rational side help you when making decisions.

Other important symbols contained in "The Judgement" card:

1. The **pennant emblazoned with a cross** is an apocalyptic symbol, from the vision of St. John.
2. The **dead rising from the grave** symbolize man's awakening and disillusionment.

An excess of color   A lack of color

55

The World 21

The number of this card in Tarot is 21 (3 x 7), and it closes the Major Arcana. The main idea expressed in this card is of

being bound to the material world.

Description

A semi-nude female figure, draped in a red scarf that conceals her genitals (thus signaling a lack of innocence, as opposed to the figure in the Star), dances, holding two wands that represent all the power and knowledge of the inner and outer worlds. She is surrounded by a laurel wreath that is bound at the upper and lower ends with ribbon, in the shape of the symbol of infinity. The very circle surrounding her is also a symbol of eternity, perpetual motion, and perfect balance.

The female figure can also be interpreted as controlling female sexuality and femininity, especially if the flowers in the wreath are considered as phallic symbols.

In the four corners of the card, there are the four angels from the vision of Ezekiel and of John that appeared in The Wheel of Fortune card: the man, the eagle, the lion, and the bull. The number 4 again symbolizes the four seasons, the four elements — producing a cyclical feeling, the inevitability of life as it goes on through eternity. The number 4 symbolizes a solid base.

This card represents the perfection of the universe and its component parts, as well as expressing the world's recognition of God. This can make the world a better place. The card symbolizes the soul and man's consciousness. Divine vision will identify the soul that knows itself.

This card sees man as a microcosm — a miniature reflection of the universe, which is the macrocosm. Motion is a sign of imperfection and incompleteness, while immobility is a sign of an absence of any needs. Thus the dancing woman is still imperfect and incomplete, and is still bound to the material world.

In a spread

In a spread, this card means preoccupation with mundane, routine, everyday things, which engender petty worries, boredom, and spiritual stagnation. It is a good card regarding material things, but is very paltry from the spiritual point of view. If the Prince of Wands appears in the spread, it could indicate events or people concerned with abroad.

If the card appears **upright**, it indicates moving house, immigration, guaranteed success, a happy sexual relationship, good luck, and meeting new people. You will definitely be successful in the future — and you will be rewarded for this. You will travel extensively, and may even decide to live in another country.

If the card appears **in reverse**, it symbolizes the inability to complete tasks, a feeling of alienation, difficulties, hopelessness, delays, and failures. Try not to succumb to apathy.

If you think and act positively, you will avoid getting into a rut.

Other important symbols contained in "The World" card:
1. The **four beasts of the apocalypse** symbolize the signs of the Zodiac — Scorpio (water), Leo (fire), Taurus (earth), and Aquarius (air).
2. The **dancer** is reminiscent of the Indian god Shiva, who activates the material world.
3. The **laurel wreath** represents the womb, from which the dancer will emerge when she is ready to break her material ties and reach the spiritual world.
4. The **silk scarf** that conceals the dancer's genitals symbolizes the androgynous nature of the dancer, meaning that the spiritual world is equally accessible to both sexes.
5. The **sticks** symbolize magic wands, indicating that man himself holds the key to his own enlightenment.

An excess of color   A lack of color

The Fool 22

The number of this card in Tarot is 0, but it can sometimes be 21 (without a change in its meaning), in which case "The World" card is 22.
The main idea expressed in this card is

"All options are open."

Description

The card depicts a light-footed youth walking along a high mountain path toward the very edge of a precipice, looking up at a mysterious point in the sky in a carefree manner. The sun illuminates his path from behind. Nothing controls him and he feels no fear. These are the distinguishing characteristics of the fool, who does not even realize that he should fear danger. He has not decided which direction to take, and the dog jumping beside him seems to be either asking him the way or warning him of the yawning abyss ahead. Despite the seemingly imminent danger, the card gives no indication of terror, since there is an element of inherent protection and trust here that guards the young man from danger.

The figure of the young man is spiritual, beyond the material preoccupations of the world. This can be seen in the careless way he holds the staff with the bundle containing material things. He does not care too much about them. In his other hand, he holds a white rose, a symbol of purity. His arms are open to the world.

It is impossible to guess what is going to happen. He may well come to a halt at the edge of the cliff, but may just as easily plunge down into the ravine: this symbolizes freedom of choice, the open options that characterize this card. He is seeking human experience, no matter what the consequences — good or bad.

There are hints of future success in the feather and laurel leaves on his head: basically, wherever he turns, whatever he chooses, he will be successful. Under no circumstances must the Fool be interpreted as stupid. The young man, who is highly intelligent, actually represents the court jester, who, with his wit and sharp tongue, would entertain, tease and satirize the people and events at the royal courts. In fact, the Fool is the source of the Joker in the modern card deck.

Another interpretation of the Fool is that of "Madman," who was considered a kind of saint and could therefore not be hurt or attacked. The Fool — or Innocent — was sometimes thought of as the person who heralded the advent of spring, similar to the Greek god, Dionysos.

In a spread

In a spread, this card is of great importance, since no matter what has preceded it, it interrupts the previous trend and opens up new options and vistas — often, but not always, positive ones.

If the card appears **upright**, it indicates that anything is possible: apathy, boredom, a tendency toward addiction or insanity — but not too much. You may enjoy new beginnings without being weighed down by residual knowledge and experiences from the past. In the future, you must guard yourself from extremes of emotions leading to profligacy, madness, and manic behavior. Don't jeopardize your chances by succumbing to inebriation or delirium.

If the card appears **in reverse**, it emphasizes all the negative aspects, such as total apathy and stagnation. Let your conduct be normal and rational in the future, and not completely devoid of caring and involvement. See that your attitude toward others is not one of condescension.

Other important symbols contained in "The Fool" card:
1. The Fool's **serene expression** and **sure footing** symbolize his unwavering belief in a higher power that will not forsake him.
2. The **rose** is a symbol of honesty and innocence.
3. The **bundle** symbolizes the paucity of the Fool's possessions, and the minimal value he places on them.
4. The **laurel wreath** indicates past triumphs and achievements; the youth could actually stop now and "rest on his laurels," if he chose to.
5. The **crimson feather** reminds us that the Fool is, in spite of everything, human, and as such, subject to human passions and impulses (this is the significance of the color red).

An excess of color   A lack of color

The 78 Cards
The Minor Arcana

The 56 cards of the Minor Arcana are divided, as we know, into four suits: cups, wands, pentacles and swords. Each suit contains ten cards numbered from one (Ace) to ten, with a numerological significance. Three additional cards in each suit are the "court cards" — King, Queen, and Prince; and last but not least, there is a Knight card.

In other words, we have 40 "numerological" cards and 12 court cards (which are parallel to the 12 signs of the Zodiac). In addition, there are four knight cards, whose main meaning is "a new path" or "unexploited ability."

We will briefly survey the significance first of each set, and then of each of the 56 cards, and their meanings. Most of the cards have a double meaning — when they are in upright position, and when they are in reverse (or positive and negative). Some of the cards only have one meaning — either positive or negative.

The Cups Suit

This suit represents the element of water in nature, and therefore the emotional world, the relationship between the members of a couple, intuitive ability and the ability to share with one's mate. The cards are extremely important in questions concerning happiness and love, and the fulfillment of one's expectations from life.

The Cups suit is parallel to the Hearts suit in the regular playing card deck.

The Wands Suit

This suit represents the element of fire, and therefore the person's abilities and talents. It is very important for identifying inhibitions and inner obstructions, as well as pressures from the past, and for understanding the person's inner equilibrium and his status vis-à-vis his surroundings.

The Wands suit is parallel to the Clubs suit in the regular playing card deck.

The Pentacles Suit

This suit represents the element of earth, and it is therefore connected to practical things like property, the power to implement things, creativity, health, will power and so on. As this suit has many ups and downs, it is very important to see where the card is located in the spread.

The Pentacles suit is parallel to the Diamonds suit in the regular playing card deck.

The Swords Suit

This suit represent the element of air, and although it ostensibly deals with logic, common sense and decisiveness, it is a difficult suit with multiple meanings. This is because when any of its cards is interpreted, the state of the other cards in the spread must be taken into consideration. To a certain extent, this is the suit that indicates the person's fate.

The Swords Suit is parallel to the Spades suit in the regular playing card deck.

The Knights Cards

The four Knights cards represent life's "Jokers," which provide us with new options. They will be discussed separately.

Ace of Cups

The name of this card in a regular deck is the

"Ace of Hearts."

The card symbolizes a new step induced by emotional motives.
It is always a **positive** card.

Description:

A delicate hand emerges from a cloud, holding a cup from which five jets of water flow into a serene lake in which water lilies grow. A dove bearing a ceremonial wafer marked with a cross flies down toward the goblet.

The hand symbolizes gentleness, and the cup is a reference to the Holy Grail, which gives its bearer superior powers. The jets of water represent the five senses, and the lake into which they flow is a symbol of man's subconscious and the Universe. The dove represents optimism and spirituality. The water lilies also have a positive symbolic meaning.

In a spread

In a spread, the Ace of Cups means a new beginning in the emotional realm that occurs as a result of heart rather than mind, emotion rather than logic. It means love, happiness, romance, fertility, and intense emotions.

If the card appears **upright**, you will encounter a will of steel and realize that the law cannot be bent.

If the card appears **in reverse**, you may be surprised when someone else changes his tack.

Other important symbols contained in the "Ace of Cups" card:

1. The **wafer** symbolizes purity.
2. The **cup** is a symbol of the Holy Grail, which confers divine powers on its holder.
3. The **hand** symbolizes a soft and gentle action.

An excess of color 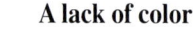   A lack of color

Two of Cups

The name of this card in a regular deck is the

"Two of Hearts."

The card symbolizes love and successful partnership.
It is a **positive** card in the realm of relationships.

Description

A youth and a maiden, hands outstretched, exchange cups as a token of love and fidelity. They wear crowns of flowers: his are red, a symbol of lust, and hers are green, a symbol of virginity and immaturity; these are opposing but complementary symbols, a characteristic of the card. Above them, two eagle's wings emerge from a lion's head on a staff around which two snakes are coiled — one symbolizing good, the other evil. The lion's head symbolizes lust, but this is tempered by the spiritual nature of the wings. The cups symbolize objects charged with the energy of their holders.

In a spread

In a spread, this card portends love, success, satisfaction, and enjoyment, with particular emphasis on mutuality and partnership, as well as cooperation with those around. It signifies love, harmony, intense emotions, relationship, family, and compromise.

If the card appears **upright**, it augurs well in the realms of romance, business, pleasure, status, and finance.

If it appears **in reverse**, you will have passionate experiences.

Other important symbols contained in the "Two of Cups" card:
1. The **maiden's robe** represents purity.
2. The **maiden's shoes**, which are blood-red, represent lust.

An excess of color    A lack of color

Three of Cups

The name of this card in a regular deck is the

"Three of Hearts."

The card symbolizes celebration.
It is a both a **positive** and a **negative** card.

Description

Three beautiful young girls, clad in richly colored garments, dance and frolic sensuously in a garden filled with fruit and flowers (a symbol of "live for today"). Their robes symbolize happy occasions and celebrations, while their raised cups represent wine. The scene, which depicts youth, joy, voluptuousness, pleasure, and vanity, is a tribute to Bacchus, the god of wine.

In a spread

In a spread, this card indicates festivities, gaiety, and sensual pleasures. It is a mischievous card, symbolizing carefree, uncommitted fun.

If the card appears **upright**, it means love, happiness, healthy sexuality, and freedom. If you are in the armed forces, you may receive an unanticipated promotion.

If the card appears **in reverse**, it means instability, promiscuity, and pleasure-seeking. The card also promises healing, closure, and comfort.

Other important symbols contained in the "Three of Cups" card:
1. The **blue background** symbolizes joy and optimism.
2. The **maidens' dance** is reminiscent of the wine dance of the god Bacchus, which is replete with debauchery.

An excess of color    A lack of color

Four of Cups

The name of this card in a regular deck is the

"Four of Hearts."

The card symbolizes rejection.
Its interpretation depends on its position in the spread.

Description

A young man, arms folded and sitting cross-legged under a tree, stares indifferently at three cups arranged on the ground opposite him. A hand issuing from a cloud offers him another cup, but he ignores it. Despite his lowered glance and sullen expression, which symbolize rejection and unwillingness to cooperate, the greenery, bright clothes and blue sky can be viewed as positive, optimistic symbols.

The three cups may indicate a situation of abundance, which explains why the fourth cup does not interest him. His apathy may stem from the fact that he has achieved his goals. Alternatively, it may be a result of listlessness, sloth, or boredom. The position of the card in the spread will reveal the answer.

In a spread

If the card appears **upright**, it indicates vicissitudes.
If the card appears **in reverse**, you may have a feeling about something about to happen.

> **Other important symbols contained in the "Four of Cups" card:**
> 1. The **hand holding a cup** symbolizes an opportunity that is being offered the youth.
> 2. The youth's **crossed legs** and **folded arms** represent stubborn rejection.

An excess of color    A lack of color

Five of Cups

The name of this card in a regular deck is the

"Five of Hearts."

The card symbolizes despair, the half-empty glass. It is a patently **negative** card. The number 5 symbolizes the Pentagram — the symbol of man — and contains the element of despair.

Description

A black-cloaked figure, head bowed and face mainly concealed, looks down at three overturned cups from which the contents have been spilled. Behind him are two upright cups — positive signs — that he ignores. In the background are abandoned buildings and a bridge over a river. The sky is gray.

The figure is clearly mourning and despairing. It is so grief-stricken that even the two upright, intact cups cannot provide a glimmer of hope. Other symbols of hope are the bridge, which beckons the figure on to more positive things, and the color yellow.

In a spread

In a spread, this card emphasizes that although the querent is in a bad situation, he is not prepared to see any positive aspects. The card is sometimes called "unjustified despair," and the querent is not prepared to shake it off. The card has a negative effect on the surrounding cards.

If the card appears **upright**, it is a good card in the main, indicating a good marriage, as well as money in the form of bequests and gifts.

If the card appears **in reverse**, you may be surprised by the unexpected return of a long-lost relative.

> Other important symbols contained in the "Five of Cups" card:
> 1. The **two upright goblets** and the **color yellow** symbolize the fact that all is not lost.
> 2. The **black-robed figure** represents the querent, who has a pessimistic outlook.

An excess of color   A lack of color

Six of Cups

The name of this card in a regular deck is the

"Six of Hearts."

The card symbolizes memories of childhood. It is both a **positive** and a **negative** card.

Description

A quaintly dressed boy hands a cup containing flowers to a little girl in an old-fashioned, fairy-tale village. Four cups with flowers stand in the foreground, with a fifth on a low wall behind the boy, a knight's shield below it. In the background, a spear-bearing guard marches away.

The symbolism is mixed: While the cups and flowers are basically positive, the flowers inside the cups indicate missed opportunities. The costumes, houses, shield and so on are storybook symbols, taking us back to our childhood. The guard is known as the "Guard of the Threshold," whose job it is to prevent man from knowing where he came from and where he is going to.

In a spread

In a spread, the card represents past memories, not necessarily from childhood.

If the card appears **upright**, it represents happy reminiscences and a pleasant past, which led to good things.

If the card appears **in reverse**, it represents a past that did not lead to good things. Another interpretation indicates problems or hopes concerning children, and this is the one that should be applied in a spread. Furthermore, there could be an unexpected bequest.

> **Other important symbols contained in the "Six of Cups" card:**
> 1. The **children** represent past memories.
> 2. The **little boy** offering the girl a cup filled with flowers represents a former love.

An excess of color    A lack of color

Seven of Cups

The name of this card in a regular deck is the

"Seven of Hearts."

The card symbolizes illusions — in fact, it is nicknamed "Seven of Illusions."
It is a **negative** card.

Description

In the foreground, a black figure with his back to the viewer waves his arm with a dramatic flourish, as if he were a magician producing seven fantastic cups, each containing some imaginary, mystical, and tantalizing thing. The cups are shrouded in smoke, which makes them look insubstantial, unreal.

But just as a magician knows that what he produces is illusion, so the stance of the figure indicates that he is merely "seeing things." He is featureless, since his face cannot be seen, and this engenders an element of dishonesty. The purpose of the card is to trick the viewer, to create an illusion.

In a spread

In a spread, this card means idle promises, meaningless talk, illusions, fantasies, and daydreams.
   If the card appears **upright**, it indicates a lovely child, as well as plans and decisions.
   If the card appears **in reverse**, it sometimes indicates success.

> **Other important symbols contained in the "Seven of Cups" card:**
> 1. The **clouds of smoke** symbolize the illusory and deceitful nature of the card — there is no solid basis to it.
> 2. The **objects** that emerge from the cups symbolize sleight of hand and trickery.

An excess of color    A lack of color

Eight of Cups

The name of this card in a regular deck is the

"Eight of Hearts."

The card symbolizes separation, abandonment. It is a **negative** card.

Description

A figure dressed in a crimson cloak and boots turns around and abandons a two-layered structure, consisting of eight cups, which he has toiled to build. The geometric shape of the structure indicates his life work, which he is leaving behind. He is walking in a barren and rocky landscape, which hints at the unknown awaiting him. In the sky, a double moon (full and crescent) looks down at him.

In a spread, the card signifies succumbing to desperation and forsaking something in which the querent invested great effort or emotion, such as a relationship or a place. The reason for the abandonment could lie in the symbolism of the color crimson — which means passion and feeling. The negative aspects of this card can only be reversed if the next card in the spread is positive.

In a spread

If the card appears **upright**, you will marry a good-looking person.
   If the card appears **in reverse**, your happiness will be complete.

Other important symbols contained in the "Eight of Cups" card:
1. The **landscape** symbolizes an uncertain future.
2. The **full moon** is a symbol of a new beginning.
3. The **crescent** is a symbol of the end of an era.

An excess of color    A lack of color

Nine of Cups

The name of this card in a regular deck is the

"Nine of Hearts."

The card symbolizes a lack of satisfaction. It is both a **positive** and a **negative** card.

Description

A well-fed man sits jovially in front of a curtained screen, upon which nine cups are arranged. Ostensibly, he is satisfied with his lot — the complacent smile on his face attests to that. But the curtain behind him conceals something. If there were ten cups, things would be perfect. There are only nine cups. Is the tenth hiding behind the curtain, tarnishing the man's perfect happiness? Is something missing?

The positive elements are the outward satisfaction expressed by the man. The negative symbols are the ones that indicate mystery, unknown, missing things (the tenth cup) — and therefore create a lack of satisfaction.

In a spread

If the card appears **upright**, you can expect good tidings if you are in the armed forces.

If the card appears **in reverse**, you will be successful in business.

Other important symbols contained in the "Nine of Cups" card:

1. The **curtain** symbolizes something vague and unknown, as well as the element that separates the man from perfect happiness.
2. The **man** is a symbol of the external appearance of things.

An excess of color    A lack of color

72

Ten of Cups

The name of this card in a regular deck is the

"Ten of Hearts."

The card symbolizes happiness.
It is an extremely **positive** card.

Description

In the sky, a rainbow-like arc of ten cups forms a radiant, colorful pattern, indicating spiritual joy rather than material fortune. Below, a loving family gives physical expression to the happiness and satisfaction they feel: the parents stretch out their arms in a happy greeting while the children dance together. The rustic background of a hillside cottage is simple, non-materialistic, and domestic, meaning that material luxuries are not required for genuine happiness.

The card seems to indicate that true bliss comes from a conventional framework of marriage and children.

In a spread

If the card appears **upright**, a male querent can expect to marry surprisingly well.
If the card appears **in reverse**, it indicates sadness and disputes.

Other important symbols contained in the "Ten of Cups" card:

1. The **colors** of the card symbolize its optimism and joy.
2. The **landscape** also represents optimism and brightness.

An excess of color    A lack of color

King of Cups

The name of this card in a regular deck is the

"King of Hearts."

The card represents Cancer (sign of the Zodiac). It is both a **positive** and a **negative** card.

Description

A king wearing a crown and a cloak, holding a cup in his right hand and a scepter in his left, sits on a stone throne in the middle of a stormy ocean. Solitude and inner contemplation may help him overcome crises and obstacles. Around his neck hangs a golden fish, while a live fish leaps out of the water behind him. There is also a ship in the background. The fact that he sits on a solid throne on an unstable basis (water) indicates clutching at material things, come what may.

This card represents Cancer, the Zodiac sign, signifying the emotional residues each person carries from his home and family. It hints at man's tendency to withdraw into himself or into his home, and at the importance of everything domestic. People whose signs are Cancer or Pisces are particularly susceptible to this card's influence.

In a spread

In a spread, this card mainly concerns home, family, and maternal figures.

If the card appears **upright**, it foretells a loving, stable family. Somebody in authority may decide to make your life difficult. Watch out for insincere offers of assistance.

If the card appears **in reverse**, there may not be a warm family life in the offing. This card is a sign of loss.

> **Other important symbols contained in the "King of Cups" card:**
> 1. The **stone throne** represents clinging to the solidity of material things.
> 2. The **golden fish** hanging around the King's neck symbolizes the love of material things.
> 3. The **king's state of solitude** symbolizes withdrawal.

An excess of color    A lack of color

Queen of Cups

The name of this card in a regular deck is the

"Queen of Hearts."

The card represents Scorpio.
It is both a **positive** and a **negative** card.

Description

A queen sits languidly and sensuously on a throne at the shoreline, the water lapping at her feet and her blue and white, scarlet-lined cloak dipping carelessly into it. She holds an ornate cup boasting scorpion's claws and topped with a phallic tower with a cross on it, and stares at it dreamily. Her throne is decorated with mermaids, symbols of eroticism and sensuality, as, indeed, is the card in general. It represents sex, and contains many symbols of lust, passion, sexuality, and eroticism, as well as danger, power, destructiveness, and slyness. The cross represents the struggle, inherent to Scorpio, between the spiritual and the material.

In a spread

In a spread, this card indicates passionate affairs, burning sensuality, uncontrollable urges, and so on.

If the card appears **upright**, magical powers are attributed to it. This can be an indication of a spurious nature.

If the card appears **in reverse**, it portends mainly evil. However, it also points to marriage — wealthy brides and distinguished grooms.

> Other important symbols contained in the "Queen of Cups" card:
> 1. The **scarlet color** of the queen's robe is a symbol of lust.
> 2. The **scorpion's claws** are symbols of the sign of the Zodiac Scorpio, the most dangerous and erotic of the signs.

An excess of color    A lack of color

Page of Cups

The name of this card in a regular deck is the

"Prince of Hearts."

The card represents Pisces.
It is both a **positive** and a **negative** card.

Description

A dreamy youth, dressed in a hat of pale blue (the color of spirituality) and a pale blue and pink tunic decorated with a pattern of water lilies, holds a cup containing a fish and stares at it. All the card's symbolism points at the characteristics of Pisces: love, romance, sweetness, gentleness, sacrifice, creativity, inspiration, imagination and confusion. This is the card of love, with not a hint of materialism.

In a spread

If this card appears **upright**, it foretells positive things. It has a wonderful significance for romance. You have creative and emotional tendencies, as well as a rich imagination.

If the card appears **in reverse**, it foretells negative things. You do not have your feet firmly on the ground, and tend to get swept away by daydreams and fantasies. You become confused in business and money matters.

> **Other important symbols contained in the "Page of Cups" card:**
> 1. The water lilies are symbols of purity and honesty.
> 2. The fish is a symbol of luck.

An excess of color    A lack of color

Ace of Wands

The name of this card in a regular deck is the

"Ace of Clubs."

The card symbolizes a new direction.
It is a **positive** card.

Description

A glowing hand emerging from a cloud grasps a sprouting wand. In the background is a tranquil rustic scene, with a castle on a hill, which symbolizes future hope and promise. The card represents blossoming or a new beginning, and that is the significance of the buds. However, the leaves that are falling from the wand are an echo of what the Clubs suit portends: failure. Even at the beginning of the path, there are some negative signs.

The thumb running parallel to the wand signifies the determination of the querent to use his initiative and succeed in a new, creative field, and make progress. He holds the key to his own future success.

In a spread

If the card appears **upright**, it foretells a change for the good, an amicable end to a previous stage, a new beginning and mainly positive development.

If the card appears **in reverse**, a baby will be born.

> **Other important symbols contained in the "Ace of Wands" card:**
> 1. The **sprouting wand** symbolizes change, which is in accord with the natural course of destiny.
> 2. The **growing buds** are a sign of hope.
> 3. The **hand** symbolizes energetic action that double-backs on itself.

An excess of color    A lack of color

Two of Wands

The name of this card in a regular deck is the

"Two of Clubs."

The card symbolizes: "Cast your bread upon the water!"
It both a **positive** and a **negative** card.

Description

A merchant stands between two staves (wands) near the battlements of a castle, his right hand holding a globe of the world, and his left touching one of the staves. He is gazing into the distance, at a bay from where his ships have just sailed. The atmosphere is autumnal (the gray sky), and radiates uncertainty about the future: Will the ships return, laden with goods? He has, of his own free will, "cast his bread upon the water," with no promise of profit, and certainly with the risk of loss. He alone will face the consequences, good or bad.

One of the battlements contains a pattern of two red roses and two white water lilies — symbolizing the duality of a positive step with unknown results. The idyllic scenery symbolizes hope.

In a spread

If the card appears **upright**, it indicates your entrepreneurial talent, initiative, and plans. However, you may experience some minor letdowns.

If the card appears **in reverse**, you are unrealistic; without seeing what is near you, you try to peer into the unknown.

> **Other important symbols contained in the "Two of Wands" card:**
> 1. The **merchant** symbolizes future hope.
> 2. The **red roses** symbolize passion, and the **white water lilies** symbolize purity.
> 3. The merchant's **left hand**, which holds a stave, is a symbol of autumn and winter.

An excess of color    A lack of color

Three of Wands

The name of this card in a regular deck is the

"Three of Clubs."

The card symbolizes good news on the horizon. Its interpretation depends on the cards near it.

Description

The same merchant from Two of Wands now stands on the shore, among three staves, his right hand grasping one of them, and the other two forming a kind of gate behind him. He impatiently awaits his richly laden ships, whose arrival is imminent, but nothing is certain: he cannot count his chickens yet. His red cloak signifies passion, but it is tempered by the green scarf, which warns against premature jubilation.

In a spread

In a spread, this card is so uncertain that it requires the cards near it for its interpretation. The empty horizon is still a question mark: there are rumors of good news, but nothing concrete. In general, however this is an excellent card. It indicates that working together with someone else will yield dividends.

Other important symbols contained in the "Three of Wands" card:
1. The **merchant** waiting on the shore is a symbol of anticipation of riches.
2. The **yellow background** is a symbol of spring and optimism.

An excess of color   A lack of color

Four of Wands

The name of this card in a regular deck is the

"Four of Clubs."

The card symbolizes reaping the rewards. It is a very **positive** card.

Description

In the foreground stands a (wedding?) canopy of flowers supported by four staves, obviously awaiting the arrival of a joyfully gesticulating couple approaching with garlands of flowers and fruit in their hands. In the background is a substantial fortress. This card radiates a feeling of well-being that stems from a combination of the spiritual and the material, hard work and creative inspiration — as well as from cooperation and partnership (as symbolized by the couple, and the pairs of staves supporting the canopy).

In a spread

In a spread, this card exerts a **positive** influence over the whole spread. Hard work will lead to rewards. The broader significance of the card relates to the querent's home, relationships and family.

If the card appears **upright**, you will have good luck that you never dreamed of.

If the card appears **in reverse**, you can expect to have lovely children.

Other important symbols contained in the "Four of Wands" card:
1. The **fortress** is a symbol of affluence and material success.
2. The **canopy** symbolizes the culmination of achievement in the Wands suit.

An excess of color    A lack of color

Five of Wands

The name of this card in a regular deck is the

"Five of Clubs."

The card symbolizes competition, struggle, and opposition.
It is an indeterminate card.

Description

Five youths dressed in sporty costumes, each holding a large staff, are involved in a non-hostile "battle" on a green lawn, under a blue sky. There is no sign of injury or blood, and the atmosphere is that of fair play. The best man will win, without animosity or foul play. The size of the staves testifies to the fact that winning requires skill and practice.

In a spread

In a spread, this card can be seen as symbolizing internal struggles and a lack of focus. The querent may be fortified by his conflicts, or he may be defeated by them. This uncertainty affects the entire spread. If the conflicts are external, they are fair and just. Nothing underhand is involved.

If the card appears **upright**, you can expect a gamble to come off profitably.

If the card appears **in reverse**, a dispute may lead to something good.

Other important symbols contained in the "Five of Wands" card:
1. The **five youths** are a symbol of fair play.
2. The **blue sky** symbolizes an absence of negative motives.

An excess of color    A lack of color

Six of Wands

The name of this card in a regular deck is the

"Six of Clubs."

The card symbolizes victory after battle. It is a **positive** card.

Description

A horseman is depicted returning triumphantly from a battle, with laurel wreaths on his head and on his staff. The colors of the sky, his clothes, the horse blanket, and the cheering crowd are all symbols of achievement and success. This is the optimal card in the Wands suit. From here, it is downhill to failure.

In a spread

In a spread, the card implies success after a struggle against opponents (as a result of hard work and skill, not just of blind luck) and leadership. This card is wonderful for all areas of life.

If the card appears **upright**, it means that employers may no longer trust their employees. The card indicates deception.

If the card appear **in reverse**, long-forgotten hopes may finally be fulfilled.

Other important symbols contained in the "Six of Wands" card:
The **laurel wreaths** are symbols of triumph following a struggle.

An excess of color    A lack of color

Seven of Wands

The name of this card in a regular deck is the

"Seven of Clubs."

The card symbolizes self-defense.
It is both a **positive** and a **negative** card.

Description

A young man stands with his back to an abyss, staving off an attack by six people brandishing tall staves at him. His fight is desperate, with the end being one of two extreme alternatives: he will be pushed over the cliff and perish, or he will defeat his enemies and live.

The positive and negative aspects of the card can refer to either external struggles or internal conflicts, when a person has to wrestle with himself and come up with an answer, for better or for worse. He may have to justify himself or fight to the death.

In a spread

If the card appears **upright**, it means that you will triumph over your vicissitudes.

If the card appears **in reverse**, you will face struggles and quarrels in every area of your life.

Other important symbols contained in the "Seven of Wands" card:

1. The **young man** symbolizes the querent, who is under attack.
2. The **staves without their wielders** represent the uncertainty shrouding the attackers.
3. The **blue sky** and **green grass** indicate that the situation is not desperate; however, they cannot do anything about the yawning abyss.

An excess of color    A lack of color

Eight of Wands

The name of this card in a regular deck is the

"Eight of Clubs."

The card symbolizes speed and haste.
Its interpretation depends on the cards near it.

Description

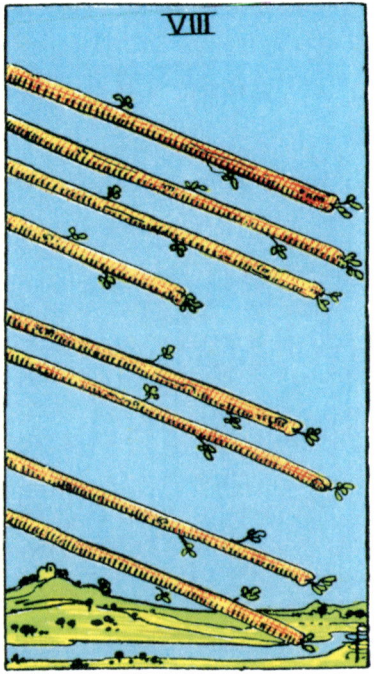

Eight staves fly through the air, in groups of four, two, and two. They symbolize actions that are taken quickly, without serious thought and consideration. The latter characteristics are seen in the tranquil landscape and the solidity of the castle on the hill in the background — and form a contrast to the freedom of the speeding staves.

In a spread

In a spread, the Eight of Wands signifies flowing and speed, which can be good and may sometimes be preferable to ponderous and long-winded decision-making. Its interpretation — whether it is positive or negative — depends on the interpretation of the adjacent cards. The card warns that you can expect to go through a rough patch with your spouse.

> **Other important symbols contained in the "Eight of Wands" card:**
> The **blue sky** symbolizes optimism, and indicates that sometimes quick action is more effective than caution and deliberation.

An excess of color    A lack of color

Nine of Wands

The name of this card in a regular deck is the

"Nine of Clubs."

The card symbolizes suspicion and lack of trust. It is a **negative** card.

Description

A man stands on guard, clutching a staff that he has torn out of a row of staves behind him. His demeanor is hostile and suspicious (expressed in his sideways glance and stoop-shouldered, defensive posture). The card emanates suspicion, hostility, alertness to danger, and lack of trust. The man's fears may not be unfounded — he may have been taught a bitter lesson in the past. There is also a hint of waiting — for something bad to happen?

Although the sky and background colors are optimistic, belying the suspected danger, the ground upon which the man stands is gray and menacing.

In a spread

In a spread, the defensiveness, inertia, and alertness to danger expressed by the card cause it to be interpreted negatively. However, it could indicate a period of transition — waiting for something, in which case the next card will be significant. This is not the best card.

Other important symbols contained in the "Nine of Wands" card:
1. The **staff** in the man's grip symbolizes a warning.
2. The **nine staves** symbolize the boundary of his territory.

An excess of color  A lack of color

Ten of Wands

The name of this card in a regular deck is the

"Ten of Clubs."

The card symbolizes failure.
It is a **negative** card.

Description

A man, bent under the burden of a bundle of ten heavy staves that threatens to come apart at any second, struggles to reach the city (or Promised Land) in the background, but it is clear that as a result of poor planning and implementation, he will never get there. Failure is assured. This is the essence of the Ten of Wands. The blue sky and pastoral scenery reinforce the fact that the man's failure is a result of his incompetence alone; nothing and no one else can be blamed.

In a spread

In a spread, it means that a person has bitten off more than he can chew, and will definitely choke. Unless a drastic change is made, failure is inevitable. The Ten of Wands offers no glimmer of hope, as did the previous cards in the Wands suit. This is not the best card.

> **Other important symbols contained in the "Ten of Wands" card:**
> The man's **clumsy posture** is a symbol of tackling a problem in an impractical way.

An excess of color    A lack of color

King of Wands

The name of this card in a regular deck is the

"King of Clubs."

The card represents Aries.
It is both a **positive** and a **negative** card — but mainly positive.

Description

An auburn-haired king (a symbol of a stormy nature) sits tense on a throne decorated with the royal symbols of lions and salamanders. He holds a staff in his right hand, and his left is poised for instant action. A salamander stands alert on the ground near the throne. The card radiates readiness to spring into action with belligerent energy.

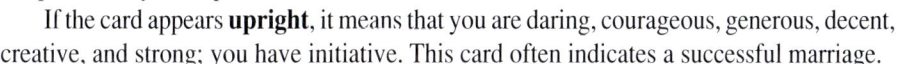

KING of WANDS.

In a spread

In a spread, people whose signs are Aries or Gemini are particularly susceptible to this card's influence.

If the card appears **upright**, it means that you are daring, courageous, generous, decent, creative, and strong; you have initiative. This card often indicates a successful marriage.

If the card appears **in reverse**, you are wild, immature, selfish, headstrong, violent, hasty, and stubborn, which can be dangerous if you are in a position of authority. You should take the advice offered.

Other important symbols in the "King of Wands" card:

1. The posture of both **king and salamander** symbolizes readiness to spring into action and attack.
2. Both **salamander and lion** are symbols of fire — the salamander is born out of fire, and Leo is a fire sign.

An excess of color    A lack of color

Queen of Wands

The name of this card in a regular deck is the

"Queen of Clubs."

The card represents Leo.
It is both a **positive** and a **negative** card.

Description

A queen sits in majestic splendor on a throne decorated with royal symbols, such as carved rampant lions. She holds a staff in her right hand and a sunflower in her left. In front of her sits a black cat; in the background, there are three pyramids. The card epitomizes innate leadership, authority, and nobility: it is her historic right to be queen, not simply a quirk of fate.

The sunflower symbolizes Leo's star, the sun, from which the queen draws her power. The cat and the pyramids are sacred ancient Egyptian signs, reinforcing the queen's right to power.

In a spread

In a spread, people whose signs are Leo or Taurus are particularly susceptible to this card's influence.

If the card appears **upright**, all the attributes of leadership, power, authority, and strength are evident. The results of things you have initiated will be good.

If the card appears **in reverse**, there is arrogance and pride, which indicate that you may be untrustworthy. You are well liked, but this may not be of any use to you.

Other important symbols contained in the "Queen of Wands" card:
The **queen's posture** and the **lions** symbolize the regal nature of the card.

An excess of color    A lack of color

Page of Wands

The name of this card in a regular deck is the

"Prince of Clubs."

The card represents Sagittarius.
It is both a **positive** and a **negative** card.

Description

A young man, dressed in fancy traveling clothes (see the boots and the feathered hat) and holding a staff in both hands, walks alone in the desert. His tunic is decorated with a pattern of salamanders (a symbol of fire – the element connected to Sagittarius). Three pyramids are seen in the background. The card expresses the love of travel, adventure, and risk that characterizes this sign.

In a spread

In a spread, people whose signs are Sagittarius or Libra are particularly susceptible to this card's influence. This is also known as the "dating" card.

If the card appears **upright**, it means that you wish to exploit your skills and talents and to broaden your horizons. It attests to your love of freedom, adventure, wandering, openness, education, wisdom, and a keen sense of justice.

If the card appears **in reverse**, you fear the future, and become apathetic. Other negative qualities are tactlessness and the urge to gamble. This card does not bring particularly good tidings.

Other important symbols contained in the "Page of Wands" card:
1. **Walking alone in the desert** symbolizes daring and adventurousness.
2. The **boots** are symbols of a lengthy walk.
3. The **hat with the feather** symbolizes hikers.

An excess of color    A lack of color

Ace of Pentacles

The name of this card in a regular deck is the

"Ace of Diamonds."

The card symbolizes taking a new step as a result of practical considerations.
It is a **positive** card.

Description

A hand emerging from a cloud holds a pentacle, a gold coin with a pentagram etched on it. Below it is a blooming, cultivated garden, with an open gate. The pentagram symbolizes man (a head, two arms, two legs). The pentacle is a material sign, which is the message of the Pentacles suit: material affairs, profits, business deals, and successful investments. The hand offers the coin; it does not clasp it.

In a spread

In a spread, this is a positive card from the material point of view, as it represents possibilities, plans, and opportunities that result from material considerations. The querent is spurred to action by thoughts of possible profits.

If the card appears **upright**, it is the best card!

If the card appears **in reverse**, you will enjoy a portion of an unexpected windfall.

Other important symbol contained in the "Ace of Pentacles" card:

1. The **pentagram** symbolizes the Spirit of God (number 1) and its material manifestation (4).
2. The **hand** is a symbol of a harmonious attitude.

An excess of color    A lack of color

Two of Pentacles

The name of this card in a regular deck is the

"Two of Diamonds."

The card symbolizes indecisiveness about a number of options.
It is a **negative** card.

Description

A juggler dressed in red teeters on one leg on a gray shore (symbolizing uncertainty), holding a rope twisted into the shape of the symbol of infinity, with a pentacle in each loop. He is trying to keep his balance, as well as to prevent the pentacles from falling. In the background, two ships ride a stormy sea precariously, threatening to sink at any second.

The entire card symbolizes instability and indecision. The symbol of infinity indicates the fact that the state of indecision can continue forever, unless a stand is taken and a decision made. The danger in which the ships find themselves is also a factor urging the man to reach a decision.

In a spread

In a spread, this is a **negative** card, as it carries a message of instability and indecisiveness, which are not necessarily the querent's fault. However, his hesitation may cause him to miss an opportunity.

If the card appears **upright**, it admonishes you not to get into a panic about problems that don't really exist.

If the card appears **in reverse**, it is not the greatest card — it warns you to be on the alert for signs of bad luck, boorishness, and injustice.

> **Other important symbols contained in the "Two of Pentacles" card:**
> 1. The **pentacles in the twisted rope** symbolize the fact that the state of indecision can continue indefinitely.
> 2. The **juggler's red clothes** mean that even difficult decisions must be made and carried out.
> 3. The **waves** and **rolling ships** symbolize the juggler being urged to make a decision.

An excess of color    A lack of color

Three of Pentacles

The name of this card in a regular deck is the

"Three of Diamonds."

The card symbolizes honor and glory.
It is a **positive** card.

Description

A young artisan stands on a platform, where he has just completed his work on the decorative arches, which contain three pentacles and a rose. Two figures, a monk and a hooded woman, are expressing their admiration of his work. The background is dark.

The card symbolizes success in one's career, and kudos from other people — praise rather than monetary reward — that increase social status. The building is a substantial sign of material success. The dark background creates a mystical atmosphere, as does the symbol of the rose, which is used by many mystical cults.

In a spread

In a spread, this card is positive, as it represents success, which may be spiritual rather than material, as well as glory and honor following personal achievements.

If the card appears **upright**, it indicates that your son is going to be famous if you are a man.

If the card appears **in reverse**, its interpretation lies with the other cards in the spread.

Other important symbols contained in the "Three of Pentacles" card:
The **monk** and the **hooded woman** represent some kind of cult.

An excess of color    A lack of color

Four of Pentacles

The name of this card in a regular deck is the

"Four of Diamonds."

The card symbolizes clinging.
Its interpretation depends on the cards near it.

Description

A miser sits on one of the crenellations of the city walls, both arms clinging to a pentacle. Each foot presses down on a pentacle, and his crenellated hat holds his fourth pentacle. The expression on his face is one of avarice and terror that his fortune might be stolen from him. He has eschewed society, which is the reason for his sitting alone on the wall.

This card symbolizes clinging to material things for security. However, the gray background indicates the opposite: the unreliability of material things as a source of security.

In a spread

In a spread, the card needs to be interpreted according to the adjacent cards. There are two possibilities for the querent: he could become a bitter miser, or he could use his hard-earned and carefully husbanded resources to initiate a new enterprise.

If the card is **upright**, you might hear something surprising but nice from a member of the opposite sex if you are unmarried.

If the card is **in reverse**, be aware of everything going on around you — especially the stumbling blocks in your path.

Other important symbols contained in the "Four of Pentacles" card:
1. The miser's **red sleeves** symbolize the lust for mammon.
2. The **pentacle** he is clutching is a symbol of his yearning for the security that material things offer.

An excess of color    A lack of color

Five of Pentacles

The name of this card in a regular deck is the

"Five of Diamonds."

The card symbolizes deprivation, lack, and poverty. It is an extremely **negative** card.

Description

Two barefoot beggars, scantily clad in rags, one on crutches, make their way through a snowstorm. Their misery contrasts shockingly with the bright, colorful, barred window, which symbolizes affluence and warmth. The wall surrounding the window is black, further emphasizing the beggars' wretched plight.

This card is the epitome of want and deprivation. The symbols of poverty clash with the opulent window, which can be seen as the home of a rich person or (worse still) as a church, to which the beggars do not have access.

In a spread

In a spread, this card is one of the worst; it has a negative effect on the entire spread, whether in material or spiritual terms.

If the card appears **upright**, you will enjoy good luck — so long as you act rationally.

If the card appears **in reverse**, your love life may not run smoothly.

Other important symbols contained in the "Five of Pentacles" card:
1. The **beggars' rags and crutches** symbolize their wretchedness.
2. The **bright window** symbolizes two things: (a) the unattainable luxury that can be seen through it, or (b) a church, which, despite its holiness, does not offer the beggars sanctuary.

An excess of color    A lack of color

Six of Pentacles

The name of this card in a regular deck is the

"Six of Diamonds."

The card symbolizes generosity.
Its interpretation depends on the cards in its vicinity.

Description

A wealthy, well-dressed merchant is handing out charity to two kneeling beggars. The expression on his face is benevolent, and he is holding a pair of scales in his left hand. His image is framed by six pentacles. The background is gray.

The merchant symbolizes something that supports the querent, while the beggars represent the querent, who enjoys some kind of support. The scales mean that the benefactor considers his generosity carefully, and may well ask for something in return. There is a hint that the querent is getting more than he deserves; he did not earn the money.

In a spread

In a spread, the card sometimes implies a legal dilemma that is likely to change the querent's status. It is unclear whether the querent is represented by the merchant or by the beggars. The perfectly balanced scales do not provide the answer to this puzzle, therefore the other cards need to be examined.

If the card appears **upright**, you are warned not to trust your feelings about what is going on at this moment.

If the card appears **in reverse**, someone may try to make you stumble on your path to advancement.

> **Other important symbols contained in the "Six of Pentacles" card:**
> The **gray background** symbolizes a situation that is not particularly dignified, and does not promise security for the future.

An excess of color    A lack of color

Seven of Pentacles

The name of this card in a regular deck is the

"Seven of Diamonds."

The card symbolizes disappointment.
It is a **positive** or a **negative** card, depending on the way it is viewed.

Description

The card may be viewed in two ways. The first, which is basically negative, depicts a vineyard laborer, leaning unhappily on his rake, surveying his miserable grape crop with disappointment. He sees the fruits of his labors come to nothing, with no profit to speak of. His investment has failed. The gloomy atmosphere of the card is reinforced by the gray skies. The second way, which is more positive, depicts the laborer resting on his rake after hard labor, but seeing the money he has earned. His work may not satisfy him, but the material rewards do.

In a spread

In a spread, the card tells of the discrepancy between the anticipated result and the actual result — invariably, disappointment ensues.

If the card appears **upright**, it indicates that a man on the verge of marriage will get a better job.

If the card appears **in reverse**, it represents negative emotions such as suspicion, worry, and a lack of forbearance.

> **Other important symbols contained in the "Seven of Pentacles" card:**
> 1. The **withered vine** symbolizes a failed investment.
> 2. **Two leaves** lie on the ground, symbolizing a failure to come to fruition.

An excess of color    A lack of color

Eight of Pentacles

The name of this card in a regular deck is the

"Eight of Diamonds."

The card symbolizes hard work that is rewarded. It is a **positive** card.

Description

An apprentice mason sits astride a bench, using a hammer and chisel (symbols of hard manual labor) to cut decorative stones, six of which hang on a nearby tree-trunk. A seventh lies on the ground under the bench. In the background stands a castle, which represents hope and promise. The gloomy colors of his clothes and of the sky symbolize how hard he has to work for his wages. However, by being economical and practical, he saves his money, which is gradually mounting up (as is seen by the rising number of pentacles on the tree). He will eventually do very well.

In a spread

In a spread, this card means that one has to work hard in order to succeed — but hard work will be rewarded. This is an important career card.

If the card appears **upright**, it warns you to watch out for a young man in your business dealings. It can also indicate a young woman of swarthy complexion.

If the card appears **in reverse**, it is a warning that financial loans will get you into trouble.

> **Other important symbols contained in the "Eight of Pentacles" card:**
> 1. The **six hewn stones** hanging on the tree symbolize monotonous labor.
> 2. The **stone** lying under the bench is a symbol of the mason's unwillingness to continue working.

An excess of color    A lack of color

Nine of Pentacles

The name of this card in a regular deck is the

"Nine of Diamonds."

The card symbolizes the fly in the ointment. It is a **positive** card.

Description

A woman dressed in fine clothes stands in a fertile vineyard, nine pentacles at her sides. On her left hand is a tough hunting glove upon which sits a bird of prey. Most of the symbols are positive and optimistic, indicating material success and financial solidity — and this is enhanced by the fact that this wealth is in the hands of a woman. The card symbolizes success and achievement. The fly in the ointment, however, is the bird of prey, which is incongruous in this delightfully rustic and tranquil scene. It serves as a reminder that nothing is perfect.

In a spread

In a spread, this card reminds us of the impossibility of achieving perfection. However, the main meaning of the card is positive, as it indicates economic prosperity.

If the card appears **upright**, it acts as a catalyst for the predictions of the other cards.

If the card appears **in reverse**, it means that your hopes will not be realized.

Other important symbols contained in the "Nine of Pentacles" card:
The **vines** and the woman's **fancy attire** symbolize success and accomplishments.

An excess of color

A lack of color

Ten of Pentacles

The name of this card in a regular deck is the

"Ten of Diamonds."

The card symbolizes wealth.
It is a **positive** card.

Description

A wealthy aristocratic family, consisting of an authoritative grandfather dressed in regal clothing, a young, handsome couple, and a child, are shown in their home — which is the castle that has featured in so many cards, usually indicating promise and hope. They symbolize old, established, solid wealth to which they were born. The hunting dogs also represent wealth, as hunting was a sport reserved for the aristocracy. The pennants on the wall add to the atmosphere of opulence. Ten pentacles are arranged in the shape of the "Tree of Life," and symbolize the accumulation of wealth in the family.

In a spread

In a spread, this card signals material possessions and wealth. If both the Nine and the Ten of Pentacles appear, it is the ultimate sign of economic prosperity.

If the card appears **upright**, it is an indication of your residence — its interpretation depends on the other cards in the spread.

If the card appears **in reverse**, you may participate in some kind of event that will bring you luck — or the opposite.

> Other important symbols contained in the "Ten of Pentacles" card:
> The **three generations** shown in the card symbolize the continuity of the family's wealth.

An excess of color    A lack of color

King of Pentacles

The name of this card in a regular deck is the

"King of Diamonds."

The card represents Capricorn.
It is both a **positive** and a **negative** card.

Description

The card depicts a richly dressed king sitting on a decorated throne, ostentatiously displaying his wealth and position. On his feet are the armored boots of a knight, another symbol of his status. The card is crowded with an exaggerated abundance of symbols of wealth, representing the king's haughtiness, even though he tries to hide this by his "modestly" downcast gaze. His castle stands in the background, yet another symbol of opulence.

The characteristics associated with the card are achievement-orientation, seriousness, responsibility, ambitiousness, the pursuit of honor and fame, conformity, materialism, and careerism.

In a spread

In a spread, people whose signs are Capricorn or Taurus are particularly susceptible to this card's influence.

If the card appears **upright**, it indicates far-reaching material success, security, and prosperity. It represents figures of authority such as employers, professors, and people in the commercial world. It can also indicate a man of swarthy complexion.

If the card appears **in reverse**, it means small-mindedness, bureaucracy, and the danger of the tax authorities confiscating property. It warns you to be on the alert for a malevolent elderly person.

Other important symbols contained in the "King of Pentacles" card:
1. The **bunches of grapes** decorating the king's robes symbolize fertility and prosperity.
2. The **roses** adorning his crown also symbolize fertility and prosperity.

An excess of color    A lack of color

Queen of Pentacles

The name of this card in a regular deck is the

"Queen of Diamonds."

The card represents Taurus.
It is both a **positive** and a **negative** card.

Description

A beautiful, feminine queen sits relaxed on a throne decorated with fruits and flowers in the middle of a natural landscape, surrounded by green grass, streams, leaves, and flowers. In the lower right corner is a rabbit. All the earthly images symbolize the earth's bounty and fertility, and represent material things such as houses and plots of land, which are connected to the earth. The queen radiates serenity, physical love, art, and beauty. The characteristics associated with the card are physicality, love of comfort, refined artistic taste, sensuality, and practicality.

In a spread

In a spread, people whose signs are Taurus or Cancer are particularly susceptible to this card's influence.

If the card appears **upright**, it means that all aspects of your life are stable. A wealthy relative may be feeling generous, or a very good marriage may be in the offing. The card can also indicate a woman of swarthy complexion.

If the card appears **in reverse**, it means that you jeopardize your economic security as a result of pursuing your desires. There may be some kind of disease lurking in the future.

> Other important symbols contained in the "Queen of Pentacles" card:
> 1. The **symbols of the earth** — the vegetation, water, and so on — represent fertility.
> 2. The **rabbit**, too, is a symbol of fertility.

An excess of color    A lack of color

Page of Pentacles

The name of this card in a regular deck is the

"Prince of Diamonds."

The card represents Virgo.
It is both a **positive** and a **negative** card.

Description

PAGE of PENTACLES.

A handsome youth stands in an enchanted landscape, holding a pentacle. However, he is oblivious to his surroundings, as his attention is focused on the pentacle, which he is scrutinizing critically. His red hat symbolizes lust, while his brown boots are a sign of the element of earth. He is seeking his way in the material realm.

In a spread

In a spread, people whose signs are Virgo or Pisces are particularly susceptible to this card's influence.
The interpretation of the card depends on its position.

If the card appears **upright**, it means that you are energetic, orderly, down-to-earth, pure and disciplined. The card is especially appropriate for young men in the military. It can also indicate a young man of swarthy complexion.

If the card appears **in reverse**, it indicates narrow-mindedness, and a hypercritical, choosy, and fastidious nature, which prevents you from taking the initiative. It warns you to be on the lookout for situations leading to humiliation and even robbery.

Other important symbols contained in the "Page of Pentacles" card:

1. The youth's **analytical gaze** symbolizes his practical, critical, and fussy nature.
2. The fact that he **ignores the landscape** represents his tendency to focus on details rather than on the whole.

An excess of color 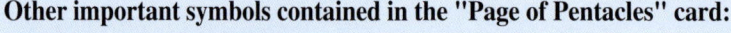   A lack of color

102

Ace of Swords

The name of this card in a regular deck is the

"Ace of Spades."

The card symbolizes a sharp turnabout.
It is a **positive** card.

Description

A hand emerging from a cloud grasps a blue and white sword aggressively, pointing it upward. It is such a powerful gesture of determination and initiative that six golden sparks fly. On top of the sword is a crown from which olive leaves (a symbol of authority, security, and peace) and a palm frond (a symbol of victory and success) dangle. It is a sign of upward mobility, with no regrets, and no backward glances at the rocky, obstacle-ridden landscape below. The card symbolizes positive, correct decisions.

In a spread

If the card appears **upright**, it represents the extremes of wealth and poverty. It means that you have made an important decision or turnabout, quite extreme in nature, and have forcibly opened a new door or started on a new path. It was your decision, and as such is your responsibility alone.

If the card appears **in reverse**, it warns that if you aren't careful, your marriage could break up because of your own impulsive behavior.

Other important symbols contained in the "Ace of Swords" card:

1. The **sword** is a symbol of immediate action.
2. The **crown** represents the victory that is the consequence of that action.
3. The **cliffs** and **rocks** on the horizon symbolize a bumpy road.

An excess of color    A lack of color

Two of Swords

The name of this card in a regular deck is the

"Two of Spades."

The card symbolizes the calm before the storm. It is a **negative** card.

Description

A blindfolded woman sits on a stone seat with her back to the ocean, where there are rocky reefs and stormy breakers, symbolizing an approaching storm. Her crossed arms hold two long swords, which she is trying to balance. A crescent moon (symbolizing a lack) hangs in the sky. The card expresses an atmosphere of imbalance, powerlessness, impotence, stagnation, inability to act, foreboding, and fear of the unknown. The gray of the sky, the bench, and the blindfold add to the gloom. There is a storm approaching (as symbolized by the precarious balance of the swords), but the figure can do nothing about it.

In a spread

In a spread, the card indicates a dire situation.

If the card appears **upright**, it means that you are paralyzed by indecision, and therefore take no action, despite the magnitude of your problems, which threaten to crush you. However, it also foretells gifts and assistance from people in high places for someone who needs it.

If the card appears **in reverse**, it warns you to watch out whom you deal with — there are plenty of con men around.

> Other important symbols contained in the "Two of Spades" card:
> 1. The **blindfolded woman** symbolizes the inability to take action.
> 2. The **crossed swords** indicate an unchanging, stagnant situation.

An excess of color    A lack of color

Three of Swords

The name of this card in a regular deck is the

"Three of Spades."

The card symbolizes sorrow and heartbreak. It is an extremely **negative** card.

Description

A red heart, pierced by three swords, is suspended in the sky. Rain is pouring from the clouds, and the background colors are gloomy, indicating heartbreak. The heart symbolizes man's psychological world, while the swords represent sorrow and emotional crises.

In a spread

In a spread, this card indicates vicissitudes and events that hurt the querent deeply. However, they are not of a physical nature, such as man-made or natural disasters; they are of an emotional nature (such as grief) and, although they are terrible for the querent, he can get over them in time. If the clouds move on, there is a chance of recovery. The adjacent cards are important for the interpretation.

If the card appears **upright**, it represents abandonment by a lover.

If the card appears **in reverse**, it means that you will run into someone you treated badly in the past.

Other important symbols contained in the "Three of Swords" card:

The **gloomy colors** show that the **swords** are not Cupid's arrows, but rather symbols of true heartbreak.

An excess of color    A lack of color

Four of Swords

The name of this card in a regular deck is the

"Four of Spades."

The card symbolizes stagnation.
Its interpretation depends on the other cards in the spread.

Description

A dead knight lies on his burial slab, his hands in a position of prayer, symbolizing hope for a better future. On the gray wall next to him hang three swords, reminders of his achievements; however, they are no longer of any use. Below him lies another sword, almost hidden in the yellow background. It is a sign that it could be drawn and used to achieve great things in the future. In the brightly colored stained glass-window, one of the figures echoes his gesture of prayer. The sword and the window are symbols of hope.

The card symbolizes powerlessness, inertia and stagnation.

In a spread

In a spread, it is not the best card.

If the card appears **upright**, it indicates that you have come up against a situation in which you are powerless to do anything (or perhaps you do not want to): it could be in a relationship, or because of an illness or a strike.

If the card appears **in reverse**, it means that you will enjoy a measure of success if you manage your affairs wisely.

> **Other important symbols contained in the "Four of Swords" card:**
> 1. The **dead knight** symbolizes inaction and stagnation.
> 2. The **bright colors** of the stained-glass window symbolize a positive future.

An excess of color  **A lack of color**

Five of Swords

The name of this card in a regular deck is the

"Five of Spades."

The card symbolizes relinquishing profits, sharing the loot, losses.
It is a **negative** card.

Description

The central figure, a man holding three swords, with two more lying on the ground at his feet, symbolizing surrendered property or achievements, gloats over two defeated enemies, who walk away from him in despair and pain (these symbolize the querent). In the background, there is a gray, stormy sea, and the sky is filled with wild, gray clouds, symbolizing troubles and problems. The figure symbolizes the losses sustained by the querent.

In a spread

In a spread, the card indicates that the querent will have to give up some of his hard-earned profits, or compromise with others, even though the achievements are yours. He has to face defeat, although technically he was the winner.

If the card appears **upright**, it means that your property is in jeopardy.

If the card appears **in reverse**, it represents sadness and bereavement.

Other important symbols contained in the "Five of Swords" card:
1. The **figure holding the swords** symbolizes the querent's adversaries, who defeat him.
2. The **retreating figures** symbolize the querent, who is compelled relinquish his property/achievements (the swords) to his opponent.

An excess of color    A lack of color

Six of Swords

The name of this card in a regular deck is the

"Six of Spades."

The card symbolizes getting out of trouble. It is a **positive** card.

Description

A boatman ferries a woman and a child (symbols of the querent) away from danger to the safe shore in the distance. The stormy sea on the lower right symbolizes danger, while the calm blue sea and the greenery in the distance represent a safe haven and optimism. The gray skies are a reminder that the woman and child have not yet reached safety: hope exists, but there is still an element of the unknown.

The card expresses the positive factor of helping people in need. The boatman has exchanged his six swords for one oar in order to help others.

In a spread

In a spread, the card means that the querent has run into a difficult situation and is in distress, but someone will throw him a "life-jacket" in order to save him.

If the card appears **upright**, it means that you will undertake a pleasant journey.

If the card appears **in reverse**, you will not achieve the hoped-for results of a legal procedure in which you are involved.

Other important symbols contained in the "Six of Spades" card:
1. The **boatman** represents the querent's "life-jacket."
2. The **gray skies** symbolize uncertainty.

An excess of color    A lack of color

Seven of Swords

The name of this card in a regular deck is the

"Seven of Spades."

The card symbolizes slyness and guile.
It is basically a **negative** card.

Description

A serious card which is sometimes called "The Traitor," it depicts a figure dressed in erstwhile "Turkish" military uniform sneaking away from an army camp (represented by the tents and pennants in the background) with an armful of swords — five — looking back greedily at two he was unable to carry. The latter is a symbol of a deed that was carried out in an incomplete and unsatisfactory manner. The scene radiates slyness, deception, treachery, guile, cunning, and stealth. The red color of his fez and boots symbolize lust for mammon and selfishness.

In a spread

In a spread, this card could serve as a warning to the querent that he may be facing treachery; in this case, the card has a positive aspect about it. Overall, however, the card is negative, because of the connotations of evil stratagems, treachery, and cunning.

If the card appears **upright**, this can be auspicious, since it indicates a tranquil, financially comfortable, rustic existence.

If the card appears **in reverse**, it warns you not to scoff at or ignore advice you are given — it would be your loss.

> **Other important symbols contained in the "Seven of Swords" card:**
> 1. The figure's **"Turkish" garb** symbolizes the shady, primitive individuals who hovered around military camps, trying to steal equipment.
> 2. The **five swords** represent booty that does not belong to the running figure — he simply stole it; he did not win it in battle (as in the "Five of Swords" card).

An excess of color    A lack of color

Eight of Swords

The name of this card in a regular deck is the

"Eight of Spades."

The card symbolizes fetters and bonds.
It is a **negative** card.

Description

A blindfolded, bound woman, dressed in clothes reserved for those sentenced to death and surrounded by a "fence" of eight swords, stands with one foot in a puddle of water and the other on the ground. This means that she has not resigned herself to her fate. Visible through the swords is a castle, which, together with the gloomy sky, adds to the wretchedness of the scene.

The card represents a difficult situation, symbolized by bonds, fences and limitations. The horizontal row of five swords represents the woman's past deeds, and indicates that she alone is responsible for her plight. The three randomly placed swords indicate the future, which is unknown.

In a spread

In a spread, the card represents a serious crisis over which the querent has no control, and that he cannot avert, unless others help him.
 If the card appears **upright**, it warns you to watch out for malicious gossip about you.
 If the card appears **in reverse**, a relative of yours will leave.

> **Other important symbols contained in the "Eight of Swords" card:**
> The **bound and blindfolded woman** symbolizes a difficult situation.

An excess of color  A lack of color

Nine of Swords

The name of this card in a regular deck is the

"Nine of Spades."

The card symbolizes worry.
It is a **negative** card.

Description

A woman sits up in bed, covering her face, petrified, as if she has just woken up from a nightmare. Nine swords hang horizontally on the wall next to her, not touching her — which may indicate that her fear is groundless — but possibly posing a threat, like the sword of Damocles. Her bedcover is patterned with the Wheel of Fortune, indicating the vagaries of fate. On the side of her bed is a scene of fencers, which adds to the sword motif. The background is black, enhancing the foreboding.

The card symbolizes fears, which may be groundless, as they may be based on feelings and not on facts.

In a spread

In a spread, the querent may experience fear, but it is quite liable to disappear, leaving him in control of the situation.

If the card appears **upright**, it is not particularly fortunate. It points at religious functionaries.

If the card appears **in reverse**, your suspicions about a person of dubious repute are completely justified.

Other important symbols contained in the "Nine of Swords" card:

1. The **woman's position** symbolizes fear of the future.
2. The **black wall** symbolizes fear.

An excess of color    A lack of color

Ten of Swords

The name of this card in a regular deck is the

"Ten of Spades."

The card symbolizes disaster, destruction and catastrophe.
It is an extremely **negative** card.

Description

A bleeding corpse, pierced from head to toe with nine swords, lies face down on the bank of a river. (The tenth sword is stuck in the ground next to the person's head — a faint glimmer of hope?) The black sky augments the misery of the scene. The fact that the person has been stabbed in the back signals betrayal and ambush. The river and the blue of the dawn indicate that life goes on, and that the disaster shown here is not connected with the rest of life.

This card is the most destructive in the whole Tarot deck.

If it appears in a spread, its effect is inevitably felt throughout, no matter how positive the surrounding cards are. However, although it symbolizes a desperate, terminal situation, the card does not foretell death. The card is the epitome of failure.

If the card appears **upright**, it can mean incarceration in certain cases. For a woman, it is an indication of betrayal by people close to her.

If the card appears **in reverse**, it means that a warrior will triumph in a battle — and profit financially from his victory.

> **Other important symbols contained in the "Ten of Swords" card:**
> The **corpse** symbolizes a desperate, destructive, and no-hope situation.

An excess of color    A lack of color

King of Swords

The name of this card in a regular deck is the

"King of Spades."

The card represents Libra.
It is both a **positive** and a **negative** card, depending on the adjacent cards.

Description

A purple-clad king sits on a tall throne, the sword of justice in his right hand. The symmetry of the card creates a static atmosphere; the ravens, clouds, and tall, unmoving trees are threatening. The color purple is the royal and divine color, indicating supreme wisdom and power of judgment, while the green hill is a sign of optimism. The card represents impartiality, the ability to see both sides of the coin, balance and harmony to the point of inertia, artistic tendencies, and powers of reconciliation.

In a spread

In a spread, the interpretation of the card depends on the adjacent cards. However, the legal aspects of the card — of law courts and cases, legal counseling, labor laws, etc., should not be ignored during the interpretation. People whose signs are Libra or Gemini are particularly susceptible to this card's influence.

If the card appears **upright**, you will enjoy balance and harmony. The card represents people in the professions.

If the card appears **in reverse**, you will suffer from indecision that prevents you from taking action. The card warns you to watch out for someone who is out to harm you. If you are involved in a legal battle, cut your losses and get out as soon as possible.

> **Other symbols contained in the "King of Swords" card:**
> 1. The **sword** symbolizes the right to stand in judgment and execute the sentence.
> 2. The **motionless trees** symbolize impartiality.

An excess of color    A lack of color

Queen of Swords

The name of this card in a regular deck is the

"Queen of Spades."

The card represents Aquarius.
It is both a **positive** and a **negative** card, and is influenced by the adjacent cards.

Description

A serious-looking queen sits on a throne on top of a mountain, her profile facing the viewer. Her right hand holds a sword, while her left forms a simple gesture of greeting. Her robe is decorated with a pattern of clouds. The winged angel carved in her throne is one of the symbols of the Wheel of Fortune. Her elevated location symbolizes her lofty spirit. The card represents some of the Aquarius characteristics, such as simplicity, originality, and freedom of spirit.

In a spread

In a spread, the card indicates unusual occurrences and actions, originality, unexpected meetings, non-conformity, breaking conventions, independent thought, and inventiveness. It foretells some event. People whose signs are Aquarius or Capricorn are particularly susceptible to this card's influence.

If the card appears **upright**, it means that you are capable of reaching a decision. Moreover, the card represents widowhood.

If the card appears **in reverse**, it means that you are narrow-minded. You are warned to watch out for a malevolent woman who wants to harm you.

> **Other important symbols contained in the "Queen of Swords" card:**
> 1. Her **outstretched hand** symbolizes her simple, unpretentious style.
> 2. The **carved angel** represents the sign of Aquarius as it appears in the "Wheel of Fortune" card.

An excess of color    A lack of color

Page of Swords

The name of this card in a regular deck is the

"Prince of Spades."

The card represents Gemini.
It is both a **positive** and a **negative** card.

Description

A handsome youth, dressed in spotless non-military clothes, brandishes his sword belligerently at a non-existent foe. The pastoral atmosphere created by the green of the grass is tainted by the dark clouds, and the blue skies are flawed by the presence of the flock of ravens. The card expresses uncertainty, contradictions, contrasts, and change. This is emphasized by the wind blowing in one direction and the clouds moving in the other.

The characteristics of this card are lightness, curiosity, superficiality, personal charm, talent for writing and trade, and instability.

In a spread

In a spread, the card signifies the above personal characteristics, as well as changing and uncertain situations. It indicates the ability to learn from experience and make decisions.

If the card appears **upright**, you are able to progress and see the good in everything. It warns you to be on the lookout for someone who wants to meddle in your business.

If the card appears **in reverse**, it indicates ignorance, confusion, imbalance and superficiality. However, you will receive incredible tidings.

Other important symbols contained in the "Page of Swords" card:
1. The **lack of armor**, which contrasts with the youth's warlike stance, is a symbol of flippancy.
2. The **dark clouds vs. the lush grass**, and the **blue sky vs. the ravens** symbolize contradictions and opposites.

An excess of color    A lack of color

The Knight Cards

The Knight cards open new doors before us, and herein lies their importance. They are unique to the Tarot cards. (To a certain extent, they parallel the Joker cards in the regular deck).

In principle, all the knight cards can be interpreted as... a new path! Their exact interpretation lies in their location in the entire spread.

As we said before, the exact interpretation of the knight cards depends on the entire spread. In general, the knight cards are very important, especially when they come after a negative card, since they indicate a path toward rectifying the situation.

Knight of Cups

The name of this card in a regular deck is the

"Knave of Hearts."

The card symbolizes plans of an emotional nature. It can be **positive** or **negative**, depending on its position.

Description

A knight astride a daintily prancing horse holds a cup and crosses a blue river that winds between the mountains. His posture, and the horse's walk, indicate lightness and informality. The river symbolizes the boundary between the world of logic and that of the imagination, as do the opposite banks of the river (plains and mountains).

In a spread

In a spread, this card indicates your — the querent's — wishes and desires. It is still hypothetical, and you can enjoy fantasizing about what is pleasant for you, what you would like, etc., both from the emotional and the material point of view. The card indicates that a friend will visit you and, as a result, you will receive an unanticipated sum of money.

Other important symbols contained in the "Knight of Cups" card:
The knight's **winged helmet** and **winged boots** symbolize inspiration.

An excess of color    A lack of color

Knight of Wands

The name of this card in a regular deck is the

"Knave of Clubs."

The card symbolizes creative plans, impulsiveness and energy.

It can be **positive** or **negative**, depending on its position.

Description

A handsome knight gallops across the desert on a large stallion, holding a staff, and wearing a salamander-patterned robe (the symbol of the element of fire) over his armor. Is he on a romantic mission? Depicted in the card are youth, beauty, energy and daring. There are three pyramids in the background.

In a spread

In a spread, this card presents new aspects of adventure, enterprise, or creativity. Energy abounds in the shape of the galloping horse.

If the card appears **upright**, it does not promise positive things, but you should make every effort to remain within the fold.

If the card appears **in reverse**, it could mean marriage — but not necessarily a happy one.

> **Other important symbols contained in the "Knight of Wands" card:**
> 1. The knight's **good looks** represent the erotic nature of his mission.
> 2. The **salamander** motif symbolizes energy.
> 3. The **knight on his horse** symbolizes an in-between situation — between one action and another.

An excess of color    A lack of color

Knight of Pentacles

The name of this card in a regular deck is the

"Knave of Diamonds."

The card symbolizes material plans.
It can be **positive** or **negative**, depending on its position.

Description

A knight seated on an immobile horse in the middle of a plowed field holds a pentacle in his hand, as if weighing it. The card indicates weighing things up, serenity, practicality, caution, and moderation. The leafy decorations on the horse's forehead and on the knight's helmet, as well as the field, symbolize the element of earth.

In a spread

In a spread, this card indicates unexplored areas in the financial or material world. The hypothetical question about some plan, "Is it worth my while?" is asked here. The plans concern material things, not emotional ones.

If the card appears **upright**, it is an indication of a person or discoveries that are of great efficacy and use.

If the card appears **in reverse**, it can indicate that a very courageous person is out of work.

Other important symbols contained in the "Knight of Pentacles" card:
The **knight's stable seat** on the **motionless horse** symbolizes moderation and coolheadedness.

An excess of color 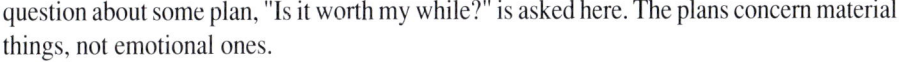 A lack of color

Knight of Swords

The name of this card in a regular deck is the

"Knave of Spades."

The card symbolizes sharp, hasty, and piercing plans.
It can be **positive** or **negative**, depending on its position.

Description

A red-cloaked knight seated on a galloping stallion with streaming mane charges into (unseen) battle, his sword cutting the air viciously. The symbols in the card do not indicate much magnanimity. There is panic (as seen in the stallion's expression), and the wind, which is blowing against the knight, is unpleasant. The gray clouds indicate uncertainty.

In a spread

In a spread, this card indicates new arenas for action in the different realms of the querent's life, and they may be sly, underhanded, hasty or conspiratorial.

If the card appears **upright**, it represents warriors — and possible heroism.

If the card appears **in reverse**, you may find yourself embroiled with someone who is your intellectual inferior, or involved in a conflict with a competitor. You will come out triumphant.

Other important symbols contained in the "Knight of Swords" card:
1. The **streaming cloak**, the **horse's mane**, and the **drawn sword** symbolize ill-intentioned haste.
2. The **red color** of the cloak is a symbol of blood-lust.

An excess of color    A lack of color

Spreads

Examples of Spreads

The examples of spreads that are presented here give the reader a rare opportunity to get a glimpse of the professional card-reader's world. In order to illustrate it, we have chosen questions pertaining to a wide range of topics that querents have addressed to the cards.

At the beginning of each spread, the question is posed, and after that, the spread is laid out. In these examples, we have used only upright cards. Six cards are chosen from the complete Tarot deck and are laid out consecutively.

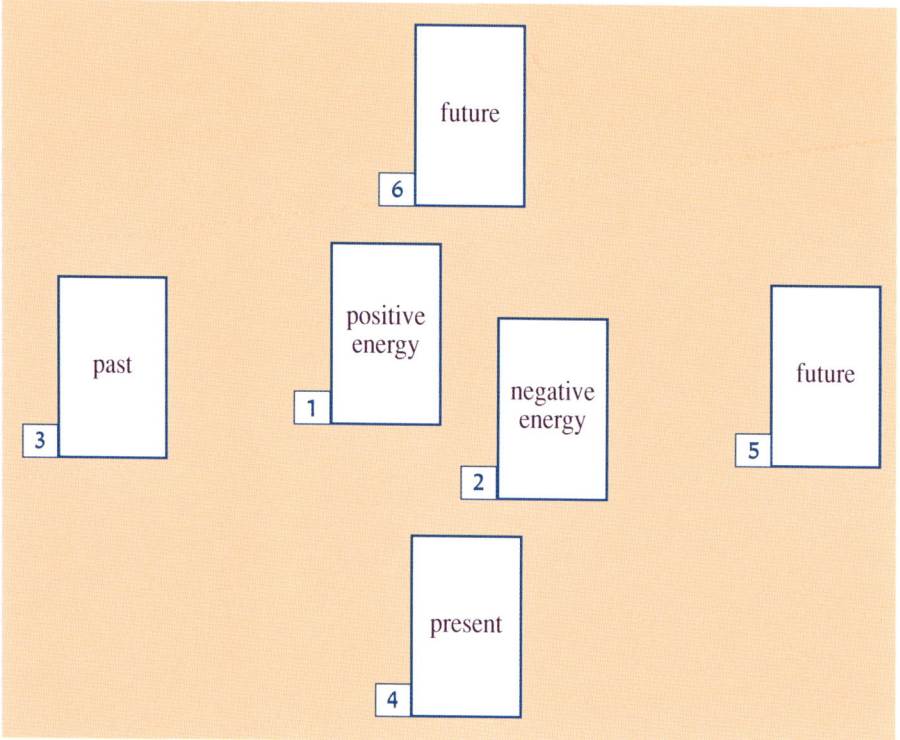

The shape of the particular spread has been chosen by us, but it is not in the least mandatory. The cards can be laid out in a straight line, in a circle or in rows. The main thing is that the cards be interpreted in the correct order. The first card that is turned over is card number 1, and the last card is number 6. Each location of the card has a specific area of interpretation:

The first two cards determine the energy that flows from the entire spread:

Card number 1 represents positive energy.
Card number 2 represents negative energy.
In other words, if the card in location 1 has a positive meaning, we will interpret it as working toward the good, the positive, regarding the question posed. If the same card appears in location 2, we will interpret it as working toward "the other side" of the querent, that is, against him.
It is customary to interpret both those cards as one unit, that is, to examine (and perhaps even write down) the meaning of each card, but to interpret both of them as a single context.

The next four cards are the time cards:

Card number 3 indicates the past.
Card number 4 indicates the present.
Cards number 5 and 6 indicate the future.
(Since the prediction of the future is the focal point of the querent's interest, and since an incorrect answer is liable to exert a deleterious influence on his decisions, two cards are used here. Some card readers prefer to label card number 5 as "the immediate future" and card number 6 as "the distant future," with the range of the future being determined by the question.)

Although each of the future cards is examined separately, the querent receives an interpretation of both of them as a single unit.

It is highly recommended that you read some of the examples that follow. First, read the question only, look at the spread, and try to interpret the cards. Prepare a sheet of paper, and, with the help of the meanings of the cards presented in the book, write down your interpretation of each card, from 1 to 6. Afterward, read the interpretation presented here and compare your interpretation to the professional one.

The more expert reader is advised to read the following chapter on professional tips and include them in the interpretations of the six-card spread presented in the present chapter.

1
Should I Tell?

"I'm a young married woman. Several months after our wedding, I realized that I had made a mistake and that the marriage was not working out. I have been considering a divorce, but I haven't spoken to my husband about it yet. To my great surprise, I have just discovered that I'm pregnant. Here is my question: Should I have the baby, hoping that it will get me and my husband together again, or have an abortion without my husband's knowledge?"

The cards were shuffled and the following spread emerged:

Now we shall interpret the cards according to their order in the spread:

Card 1: Queen of Swords

This card means that the querent should not toe the line and be a conformist; she must not adhere to concepts defined by society as the right thing to do. Rather, she should aim for what is different, original, and right for her. She must follow her heart and do things differently than is expected of her, even if this provokes raised eyebrows. However, if her partner is an Aquarius, she should think twice about her moves and decisions, because an Aquarius is the perfect partner for her.

Card 2: Ace of Wands

This card symbolizes changes in the querent's romantic life and the possible blooming of a frozen relationship. The querent should not expect a solution for her predicament to materialize out of the blue. She must calculate her moves carefully and not make hasty decisions; she must act only after considering every option. If she makes a hasty move, she might pay dearly and be forced to endure pangs of conscience and uncertainties about her choice, and these might haunt her for the rest of her life. Only if she takes the time to consider things and reach the correct conclusions will she know that the step she took was the right one.

Card 3: The Tower

This card corroborates the querent's feeling that her relationship with her husband has reached a dead end and total collapse. This card indicates a serious breakdown in the relationship. Their love life has changed, and the card indicates that clearly.

Card 4: The Magician

This card means that the present is entirely in the querent's hands. She is in control, and she alone will determine her path. From this position, she can make decisions for others and instruct them how to act. This works to her advantage. She is the one to decide about her present and future, and she has the full power to do so. Nothing can undermine this situation and she must take advantage of it.
The present situation is very positive and beneficial for her. She could not have found a better position of control or standpoint from which to clarify her present and future wishes.

Card 5: Two of Wands

This card indicates that the querent is about to make a serious investment or sacrifice in the romantic area of her life, for the sake of her future, although she does not yet know what the consequences will be. Despite her hesitations, she intends to make one of the most significant and decisive moves of her life. Although she is not certain that the move will in fact produce positive results, she wants to chance it, preferring to take a risk rather than stagnate.

Card 6: Knight of Swords

This card indicates that the querent has hidden intentions - clever and cunning ones - that might trick her unwitting partner. At the same time, the card clearly shows that despite her plans and fierce desire to do something, nothing will materialize. The querent is confused, highly emotional and under strong inner pressure to act. Still, in spite of all that, she will make no critical or significant move in the end.

2
Is This Just A Passing Crisis?

"Recently, I found out that my husband is having an affair. He tried to hide it from me, but failed. Everything pointed to it. I have a feeling that he is not just fooling around, but that he is in love: He is often confused and forgetful, and finds it hard to concentrate. Clearly, something is happening to him. Is this just a passing crisis, or is he about to leave me for his lover?"

The cards were shuffled and the following spread emerged:

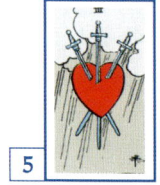

Now we shall interpret the cards according to their order in the spread:

Card 1: Page of Pentacles

The first card the querent pulled out provides some explanation regarding her relationship with her husband and her suspicion of being betrayed. The card hints at a relationship in which both parties are petty, critical, sarcastic and nit-picking. It is evident that the couple have spent years together without making real changes or introducing any novelty. Their boredom is showing, and it would not be surprising if, as a result of their unhappy life together, the husband were involved in a love affair that brought some color and flavor to his life.

Card 2: Page of Wands

This card speaks of a love affair that is either taking place abroad or is connected indirectly to another country. The querent's husband may travel abroad extensively in the framework of his job, which would provide the ideal conditions for his love affair. It is also possible that his lover is a foreigner or travels a lot. The card clearly shows that the "thing" (in this case, it is probably the husband's affair) related to another country is an obstacle in the querent's path toward the fulfillment of her goals in life. In reference to her question, it seems that it will not be easy for her to hold on to her marriage.

Card 3: Eight of Swords

In general, this card speaks of "romantic triangles," which is precisely what is troubling the querent. Since this card reconstructs the querent's past, it shows that she was either involved in a serious relationship or was associated with a person who was not available. Possibly, she was once on the other side, seeing a married man - hence her sensitivity, which reaches the point where she feels that her husband is head over heels in love. Chances are that she herself has experienced that scenario before and knows where it might lead. She might even be carrying the "romantic triangle" over from a previous incarnation.

Card 4: Ace of Swords

There is no doubt that the querent is on the verge of making an about-turn in her life; it will start with affairs of the heart, but it will drastically alter her life in general. The card indicates that the things happening in the querent's life now will bring about an extreme change.

Card 5: Three of Swords

The querent is experiencing a difficult time because her emotional world has been dealt a serious blow. She feels deep regret about the deterioration in her relationship with her husband, and feels there is nothing she can do about it. She feels that, if her husband is in fact deeply in love with another woman, whatever she does will make her look ridiculous and will not help. The immediate future is not going to be easy, and the querent should fortify herself as much as she can in order to be able to cope with it. The card clearly indicates that her present situation will cause her suffering.

Card 6: Five of Swords

If the querent was not one hundred percent certain whether her husband was having an affair or not, this card confirms it. Dubbed the "card of treachery," it indicates that there is a third party involved in their conjugal life. Now that the bitter truth has been confirmed, she must plan her next moves carefully and digest the news slowly. She must not do anything hasty because she might do something foolish. She must weigh up her course of action cautiously. If she really wants her husband back, it may not be too late. If she makes the right moves, she may well succeed

3
Is She Sincere?

"I am a widower in my fifties. I have worked hard all my life and have managed to accumulate substantial property. You could say I am wealthy. Recently, I met a woman in her thirties. She seems to be fond of me and has even expressed her love for me. Still, I'm not certain that she is sincere. I'm afraid she does not really love me, but wants me for my wealth and financial status. How can I tell?"

The cards were shuffled and the following spread emerged:

Now we shall interpret the cards according to their order in the spread:

Card 1: Knight of Wands

The querent is going through a phase of planning, not action. The card encourages creativity and energy, but this is not the time to make decisions and act on them. The young woman in his life fills him with vitality and energy, inspiring him to make plans and think of new ideas every day. However, this should be a time for planning only.

Card 2: Queen of Wands

This card provides a classic description of the querent's situation. It emphasizes the fun aspect of his affair, as well as the atmosphere of joy and pleasure, without a definite framework. That is, the card certainly does not forecast a wedding. It also warns against becoming addicted to a frivolous life of fun, living for the moment. It reinforces the querent's feeling about the future in order to get him to think about it and not let things just happen without a plan. If the querent's partner is a Leo, the card provides a clear warning that she is liable to hurt him.

Card 3: Two of Swords

This card represents the past, describing a person trapped in a destructive, non-constructive or even crumbling relationship. The only thing he can do about it is sit and watch. There is nothing he can do to change it. It may have something to do with a previous relationship in which things worked against him without him being able to do anything about it. At the same time, it is possible that it refers to a process in which his partner was involved in the past.

Card 4: Four of Cups

The key word associated with this card is "rejection." The querent is not certain that he should propose to his partner because he is not sure of her love for him, and is afraid that she is only after his money and status. He would be advised to heed this card and adopt a mode of "rejection." Hasty decisions might turn sour. He should give the present relationship more time and allow himself and his new partner the opportunity to experience new things before deciding whether he should marry her. This is not the time to make serious decisions. He should leave this for a later stage, after he has examined their relationship from various angles and learnt more about the young woman.

Card 5: The Magician

This card, which reveals the future, promises the querent that things will develop in his favor, and that he controls the romantic relationship he is in. It is he who dictates the rules of the game, and the nature of his relationship with the young woman foretells success and achievements. In the future, too, he will be the one pulling the strings. Even if he is not certain of himself at the moment and does not know whether his partner is attracted to him as a person or to his wealth, he can rest assured that his partner depends on him, and not the other way around. It is first and foremost his dominant and charismatic nature that attracts her to him.

Card 6: The Fool

This card shows that all the options in this relationship are open, and mostly for the good. The querent will determine the way things go and his control will prove to be worthwhile. He is free to choose any direction he wants. They all have a good chance to develop positively.

4
Should I Start a Business?

"I'm a very ambitious person. When I want something, I usually get it. I'm about to start a new business. I have enough money to make an initial investment, but that's all I have. Should I invest everything I have in this business? Will it work?"

The cards were shuffled and the following spread emerged:

Now we shall interpret the cards according to their order in the spread:

Card 1: Queen of Wands

This card encourages the querent by supporting his new plans. According to this card, the querent should adopt an independent and self-centered approach. He should ignore what other people think or say. If his environment is not fully supportive, he should ignore it and focus on his own abilities and ambitions, because he can go far. This is a very good card in terms of investments and profits - provided he remains level-headed and does not make serious and irreparable mistakes.

Card 2: Two of Pentacles

This card describes the querent's situation, warning him against deliberating too much. While the querent is not certain whether he should invest his money in his planned business, this card urges him to make a quick decision and not hesitate for too long, because he might find himself "stuck." This might be the worst possible situation for the development of his business or investment channels. If he wishes to start a business, he should make the correct decisions at the optimal time.

Card 3: The Chariot

Describing the querent's past economic situation, the card shows that he used to be subject to the authority of others and did not call the shots. Indeed, he enjoyed security and stability in a good position, but could not live with the fact that "he who pays the piper calls the tune." Apparently, this feeling drove him to consider starting his own business in which he would be his own boss. Independence is very important to him and, being ambitious, he will do everything in his power to attain his goals.

Card 4: Nine of Swords

The querent's present situation is tough. He has serious doubts about his financial future and is extremely anxious about his investment. This is not an easy time for him, as it is full of fears, questions and doubts. He knows that if he fails, he might find himself in a financial bind from which it will be difficult to extricate himself. He should reduce the pressure he is under and start thinking in a clear and stress-free manner, to the best of his ability. Only then will he be able to make the right decisions.

Card 5: Three of Pentacles

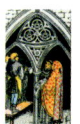
This card, which refers to the future, promises the querent that, if he invests in the business he wants to establish, he will undoubtedly earn a lot of esteem and kudos from those around him. People will think highly of him, and he will be respected and awarded high social status. However, the card does not foretell that this respectable status will lead to major financial achievements. Even if others see him as financially successful, there are no assurances that his coffers will indeed be full. The same holds for his satisfaction with life and with his personal achievements. Thus, the card predicts social status and recognition of his abilities, but nothing else - neither in the economic nor the personal realms.

Card 6: Six of Pentacles

The querent will receive massive financial backing from a particular source in the future (possibly from a family member or by winning a court case). He will move ahead, people around him will respect him, and he will earn status that far exceeds the extent of his initial investment. He will not have to work too hard for a living, and certainly not for distinguished social status and respect from others, which will come to him automatically and effortlessly.

5
Will I Be Able to Pay?

"I am a widow. My husband passed away several years ago and I have been living on social security ever since. When he was alive, he used to take care of our financial affairs. Now I want to buy a new apartment, but I'm afraid I won't be able to cope with the mortgage payments. Should I risk getting into this?"

The cards were shuffled and the following spread emerged:

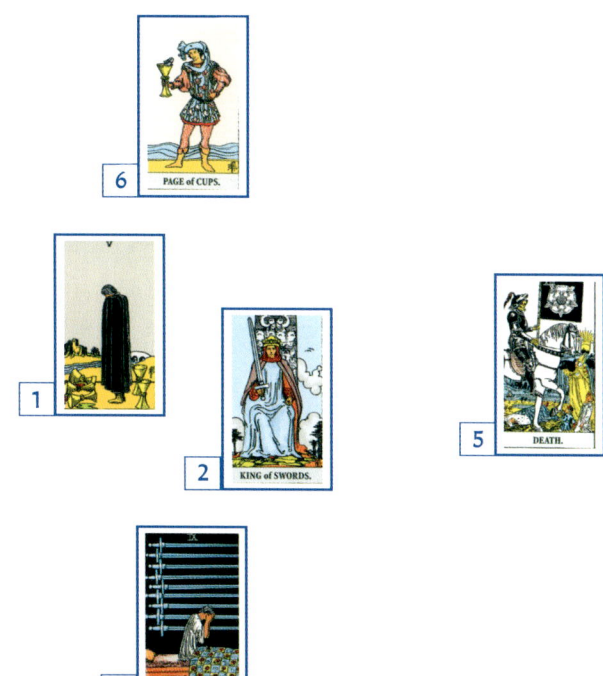

Now we shall interpret the cards according to their order in the spread:

Card 1: Five of Cups

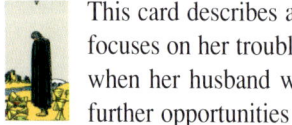
This card describes a situation of serious deliberation, indicating that the querent focuses on her troubles excessively. Even if her financial status is not what it was when her husband was alive, she must not ignore the fact that the future holds further opportunities for her. Moreover, the card indicates that the querent is in a favorable situation. The fact that she is not certain about her next move is forcing her to stop and take a good look at what she is about to do. She should take a time-out, consult relatives and experts, and examine every option before taking a step that might be detrimental to her.

Card 2: King of Swords

This card warns the querent of legal problems she might encounter. It forecasts legal deliberations, counseling or involvement in legal affairs. There may be some problem related to tax payments, debts or fines. She may not be able to meet the commitments she undertakes, hence the legal problems. The card is clearly a warning against coming into conflict with the law, although obviously not in a criminal context.

Card 3: The Fool

The querent has not attained self-fulfillment, never formulated her own worldview, and never really controlled her life. She found this situation convenient. She was not like that as a result of her husband's conduct, nor did he stifle her development. She alone chose not to develop. She had every opportunity to do so, but chose not to. Now, when she is required to make important decisions on her own, she has become aware of her shortcomings as an adult.

Card 4: Nine of Swords

The querent is experiencing a difficult time, and her fears are certainly understandable. The stress, worries and anxieties will pass once she makes a decision she can live with. There may be no real reason for her fears, and in fact, this card indicates that her fears are unfounded. However, she cannot ignore the tension she is experiencing. Even if in her heart of hearts she knows she has nothing to be afraid of, that people around her will look out for her in times of trouble, her fears and anxieties are overpowering.

Card 5: Death

This card forecasts upheaval and a change of direction for the querent. So far, she has been a passive woman, lacking control of her life, without a clear direction, and totally submissive to her husband's wishes and decisions. Pretty soon, however, everything will change. She will take charge of her life, become independent, make her own decisions and take control of her destiny. She will no longer follow somebody else's line, but will become a woman who is self-aware, liberated and assertive. The card indicates that financial resources that were previously closed to her have been released, and they represent new and revolutionary financial opportunities.

Card 6: Page of Cups

The future foretells a confused and problematic situation. The querent is not fully versed in the complexities and mysteries of the world of finance, and is liable to make mistakes. She is not fully aware of the complications of buying an apartment, and cannot assess her ability to pay out such a large sum of money as well as cope with the mortgage payments. She does not know how to make the connection between reality and real demands on the one hand, and the actual means at her disposal on the other. She tends to fantasize and allow her imagination to take over, and she is not always fully aware of the difference between fantasy and reality.

6
Who'll Get the Promotion?

I have a good job and a senior position in a large hi-tech company. My superiors are very satisfied with me and I think I'll get a promotion soon. The problem is that there is another employee who is a serious competitor for the new job. I am very stressed out as a result. Is this feeling justified? Will I get the promotion or will my rival?"

The cards were shuffled and the following spread emerged:

Now we shall interpret the cards according to their order in the spread:

Card 1: Three of Wands

This card carries a clear message. It shows that the querent is good at what he does and that he is a serious candidate for a promotion. His hard work, overtime and shouldering of responsibility are beginning to bear fruit, but the fruit is not yet safely in his pocket. He feels that he is viewed positively by his peers and superiors, and receives praise, but nothing tangible has been offered to him yet. His colleagues cooperate with him and his superiors praise him, but the job he hopes for is not yet his. The card recommends that the querent trust the positive signs he is receiving, and, above all, encourages him to have faith in promises.

Card 2: Page of Wands

This card describes a career that is somehow associated with foreign countries. Something about the querent's work involves something abroad; he may be expecting to travel or deal with import-export; alternatively, other people, events or things associated with foreign places will thwart his plans or prevent him from attaining his goals.

This card also hints that legal matters, mainly academic, such as the study of the law or a person associated with such studies, will prevent him from doing what he wants or stand in the way of his goals.

Card 3: Seven of Pentacles

This card represents the gap between expectations and their realization. It indicates that the querent has already experienced situations in which his efforts and investment did not yield the expected results. He has probably been through the experience of investing a great deal of time, effort, money or emotion, but with disappointing results.

Card 4: Nine of Cups

This card clearly shows that the querent is not satisfied with his present position, as he feels that his career is not going anywhere. He aspires to more and is suffering from a lack of interest in and boredom with what he does. He wants much more than he gets from either his workplace or his field of work. His displeasure derives more from inner feelings than from rational thinking. He may be satisfied with his salary and his economic and material situation, but his professional desires are not being fulfilled. He wants to get a promotion, in the hopes of finding new interest in his work.

Card 5: Six of Pentacles

This card indicates that, in the near future, someone - probably a work associate or superior - will take the querent under his wing, look out for him and push him forward. That person will not be doing so in his own interest or in the expectation of being rewarded, but rather because he has full faith in the querent's skills and wants to help him because he deserves it. The card foretells that the querent's future earnings or income will increase. Clearly, he will be promoted to a higher position that is far more interesting and important than his current job. It is also possible that the new job will bring esteem and status out of all proportion to the amount of effort involved.

Card 6: Ace of Pentacles

This card, which forecasts the future, shows that the querent will develop or make his way toward a new destination in life. However, it clearly shows that the querent's motivation for seeking a new start is purely economic. It appears that his financial and material motivation in seeking a more prominent position is very significant. This desire parallels his wish to find new areas of interest and more satisfaction at work.

7

Will My Daughter Have a Transplant?

"I have an eight-year-old daughter with cystic fibrosis [CF]. The life-span of children with this disease is short - the oldest ever CF patient survived to the age of 34. My daughter is presently in good shape, but I know that her only chance of survival is a heart-lung transplant. If she does not undergo the operation at a particular point, she will almost certainly die young. We have to take care of her to make sure that she is in a good enough physical condition to make it to the operation. Will we be able to do this? Will she make it at all?"

The cards were shuffled and the following spread emerged:

Now we shall interpret the cards according to their order in the spread:

Card 1: Three of Swords

The querent is in a negative emotional state and feels very frustrated because there is nothing he can do right now to alleviate his daughter's condition.

Things are not as bad as they seem at the moment, but the querent is in no position to see any light at the end of the tunnel. However, things are working in his favor: His present sorrowful mood will lead him to better things in the future. Every cloud has a silver lining.

Card 2: Knight of Swords

The querent is seeking a clever short-cut to his goal. The card indicates that he is being too hasty for his own good. It warns him against making rush decisions without thinking things through. He should avoid making hasty or frantic decisions and, most of all, he should avoid panic. He must not make sketchy, incomplete plans. He should act very cautiously and slowly in order to attain the hoped-for results.

Card 3: The Chariot

This card describes the querent's stable and safe past life in contrast with his daughter's situation. At the same time, it notes that things are not fully in the querent's control; rather they are in the hands of the medical profession, or God. The querent and his family cannot dictate the sequence of events, nor are they the only ones that can influence the child's condition. Although the querent's position is safe and sound and he is competent, his daughter's future does not lie in his hands.

Card 4: Eight of Cups

This card describes the present situation of the querent and his daughter, and indicates the difficult period they are going through in terms of health. They have no vitality. The card, that speaks of desertion, separation, or the end of an era, indicates that there is a serious illness tormenting the querent. He is in a state of emotional and mental exhaustion, and feels completely powerless. His frustration is enormous.

Card 5: Four of Swords

The immediate future does not predict much progress in the daughter's situation. She seems to be entering a period of stagnation: no progress but no deterioration either, which should be noted. Even the slightest deterioration could be devastating. The card predicts no such deterioration, a fact which should bring the querent a modicum of relief. There may be a long period of hospitalization, but only for observation or routine treatment.

Card 6: Nine of Swords

Tension, worries and anxieties will feature in the querent's life during the next six months at least. This mood of worry will not change, even if his daughter's situation improves. He is so worried about her that he finds it hard to rid himself of such feelings, even if he can clearly see an improvement in her condition. The querent is facing a difficult period, but he should remember that his feelings do not always coincide with reality and the facts. He should always be optimistic and hope for the best.

8
How Long Have I Got To Live?

"I am a 28-year-old homosexual. My parents and friends know about this. I have recently been diagnosed as HIV-positive. I've accepted the fact that I will die young, but I would like to know whether I will develop full-blown AIDS early on or at a later stage. I would also like to know how long I've got to live."

The cards were shuffled and the following spread emerged:

Now we shall interpret the cards according to their order in the spread:

Card 1: Ace of Wands

This card indicates that there is a way to improve the querent's health, provided he takes the initiative and finds ways to help himself through alternative medicine, which deals with the soul as well as the body. He should also trust his emotions more than his logic in future moves.

Card 2: Justice

Being the second card, Justice describes the querent's situation and the damage to his health, hinting that he brought this catastrophe upon himself. He was not careful enough, and his predicament is his own fault. He can, however, improve his quality of life, but it is entirely dependent on him. There is a warning here, stating that he is liable to destroy himself with his own hands. He can determine not only the quality of the time he has left, but also how long he has left to live. He can prolong his life or cut it short. The issue is how he chooses to live the rest of his life: in a good and healthy manner, or in a destructive way that will lead to an early death.

Card 3: The Empress

This card reconstructs the querent's past and indicates that he used to enjoy excellent physical and mental health. His life was happy, fortunate and successful. All this gave him a healthy basis and a good quality of life. It seems that his present state is the result of a single slip. Hopefully, his excellent mental fortitude, which served him well over the years, and is also giving him strength him now, will enable him to live a quality life during the time he has left.

Card 4: The Fool

This card shows that all the querent's options are open. The querent currently finds himself in a period of uncertainty regarding the development of the disease: He may be a carrier for a long time; alternatively, the disease may erupt suddenly; but then it may not start at all, if a cure for AIDS is suddenly found. Anything is possible, which is why the querent is advised to remain optimistic and favor a positive approach, so that his life will be good.

Card 5: Nine of Swords

The immediate future will be fraught with tension, worries, anxieties and fears. The querent is headed toward a difficult period, above all psychologically. This does not mean that his fears are necessarily justified. Still, although the querent has good reason to be afraid and worried, the disease is not expected to become full-blown at any moment. He should minimize his fears and stabilize his mental state, so that he can lead as normal a life as possible.

Card 6: Five of Pentacles

The card shows that the querent in poor mental and physical shape. Although he is in a situation of distress, he should not despair, as the previous cards indicated, because this will do him no good. He should try to remain as optimistic as he can.

9

Will My Daughter Leave Her Junkie Boyfriend?

"My daughter is seeing this junkie and it seems there is nothing I can do about it. My greatest fear is that she is taking drugs, although she denies this vehemently. She claims she is in love with the man, and it is beyond her control. All my attempts to get her to break up with him have failed. Will she ever leave him? If she does, will it be of her own volition? Should I keep trying, despite the fact that it isn't doing any good?"

The cards were shuffled and the following spread emerged:

Now we shall interpret the cards according to their order in the spread:

Card 1: Nine of Swords

This card shows that the mother's fears regarding her daughter are justified. The querent is tense and worried about what her daughter's future holds. This card clearly indicates an existing problem that should not be ignored and that should be related to. It warns that there is no room for complacency, and that action should be taken immediately, before it is too late.

Card 2: Seven of Swords

The card describes a cunning, sophisticated and treacherous move that the querent should beware of; things which might harm her are taking place behind the scenes. The daughter may be manipulating her mother into believing that she is pure as the driven snow. The mother must exercise caution and observe her daughter's actions closely in order to make sure that she is not finding ingenious ways of evading her.

Card 3: Page of Swords

This card shows that the querent's past was turbulent and unstable. Either she experienced drastic changes or she preferred superficial to profound things. This is not necessarily negative. There was probably a time in her life when it was easier for her to be superficial about certain things, instead of going into them in depth and enduring intolerable pressures. This, however, may be the source of her daughter's behavior.

Card 4: Ten of Swords

This is a very powerful card which is indicative of the mother's grim present. The current period may be the worst she has ever experienced. From her point of view, it is a tragedy. The situation she is in is disastrous and destructive, both for her and for those close to her. It is so difficult that sometimes there seems to be very little hope. The querent relates to the situation as catastrophic for her, her daughter and the rest of the family.

Card 5: Nine of Wands

The querent is having a hard time trusting her daughter, although she would like to. As long as she sends messages to her daughter, saying: "I'm watching you," she will continue feeling her daughter's alienation, hostility and suspicion. The querent will go on making carefully calculated moves, mainly because she does not fully trust her daughter. The daughter will sense her mother's attitude, and this will make it even harder for the mother to give her daughter the feeling that she trusts and believes in her.

Card 6: Four of Wands

This card assures the querent that if she persists and does not give up, her efforts will prove to be worthwhile. The extent of her future success depends on her efforts in the past. If she is persistent, aware of her daughter's moves, and on the alert, she will be able to get her away from her boyfriend and win the battle. After that, thanks to her actions and persistence, she will have succeeded in bringing her daughter back.

10
Trapped

"I feel trapped. I am madly in love with my lover, but I live with my husband and our children. I can't even think of breaking up the family because I don't want to hurt the children. However, I'm afraid that once my lover realizes that I have no intention of leaving my husband, he'll give me up and find someone else. This would leave me without love, which would kill me. Should I leave my husband and kids for my lover, or should I stay with them?"

The cards were shuffled and the following spread emerged:

Now we shall interpret the cards according to their order in the spread:

Card 1: Seven of Cups

This card encourages the querent to believe in ideas that seem unreal, imaginary and fantastic at the moment. It carries a promise that today's illusions will become tomorrow's reality. The dilemma that the querent faces makes her feel that the option of living with her lover is an illusion, an unrealistic figment of her imagination. She is such a responsible person with such a serious moral dilemma about leaving her children that she feels as if her desires will never be anything more than figments of her imagination, as if they can never be realized.

Card 2: Wheel of Fortune

This card warns the querent against changes, hinting that breaking up her home is risky. There is no way for her to know what her everyday life with her lover would be like. She cannot know that while being married to another man. A decision to divorce her husband and move in with her lover might prove risky because the magic that exists between them now might turn out to be just an illusion. She vacillates between ecstatic joy and deep despair. This period of uncertainty is not the right time to make decisions that might cost her dearly.

Card 3: Nine of Pentacles

According to this card, the querent's life used to be pleasant and peaceful. With her husband, her life progressed well and their love was honest and beautiful. It seems, however, that at a certain point, she was forced to make some kind of concession or compromise that caused her mental anguish, and it was probably for this reason that she became involved in an extramarital affair. She may have not thought much about that compromise at the time, but it seems to have had a very serious effect on her - far greater than she could have imagined.

Card 4: Three of Pentacles

The querent's position in society is very strong. She is used to accepting social norms, living by the rules. Her marriage is so conventional that the very thought of seeking personal happiness at her family's expense is foreign to her. She is so used to living according to social norms that sometimes the opinion of others is more important to her than true happiness. Much of her inability to get up and do what she desires stems from her fear of going against social norms, of what her parents and close friends might say. Her life with her husband is outwardly so comfortable and serene that she lacks the courage to break away and destroy that perfect façade.

Card 5: Justice

This card clearly shows that the querent's life with her husband has no future and that divorce is on the horizon. It warns that the divorce may not be smooth, and that there might be a series of legal proceedings. The card also hints that the querent is the only one responsible for her future, which depends on moves she makes today. Even if her future life is not easy, and even if she regrets things she did, there will be no one to blame but herself.

Card 6: Six of Pentacles

This card hints that the future will yield profit or a status that will be way out of proportion to the querent's investment. She will get more love than she gives. She will be loved, pampered and needed, while she will not give back as much love to the person she is with.

Spreads

Tips for Reading the Cards

In the following list, there are 106 professional tips gathered by well-known card-readers. These tips are helpful in focusing the interpretation by emphasizing the card combinations, or the frequency of cards in a spread. The appearance of Major Arcana cards next to each other in a spread is of cardinal importance, as is the frequency of the court cards (which are also known as royal or family cards).

When a combination of two cards is presented, for example, The Empress + Three of Cups, it means that in the spread, the Empress card was revealed first, followed immediately by the Three of Cups, when both the cards are upright. This is also the meaning regarding linking.

In contrast, when "card with..." is indicated, it means within the same spread. This is also the meaning when "appear" is written, and so on.

In the spreads you read, pay attention to the combinations of cards, and prepare your own list of significant combinations.

The List

1. The Empress + Three of Cups = pregnancy.

2. The Empress + The World = pregnancy.

3. The Empress + Ace of Wands = pregnancy.

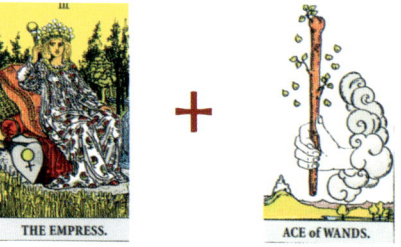

4. The Empress + a Pisces card = pregnancy.

5. When The Fool or The World appears as the first or last card in a spread, it is difficult to obtain a clear picture of the spread.

6. When three court (or royal, or family) cards from the Minor Arcana appear consecutively in a spread — King, Queen, or Prince — it means that the problems are always in the area of the family.

7. When two cards from the Major Arcana with consecutive numbers appear in a spread (12 after 11, for instance), the interpretation relates only to the second card (12) and the first card (11) is ignored. This is also the case when there are three or more consecutive cards from the Major Arcana.

8. When two cards with the same number (or description) from the Minor Arcana appear in a spread (and it does not matter how many cards it contains), for example, Eight of Wands and Eight of Pentacles, the importance of the numerological interpretation of that particular number increases. (This refers to cards number 2 to 10 in each suit only.)

9. When two cards from the same suit in the Minor Arcana appear in a spread, the importance of the suit increases. For instance, if two Pentacles cards appear, the importance of the suit increases in the interpretation of the spread. When there are four cards from the same suit in a spread containing up to eleven cards, the entire interpretation is focused on that suit.

10. The Death card does not predict death unless there are at least two cards from the following list in the spread as well: Judgement Day, Eight of Cups, Ace of Swords, Four of Swords, The Tower, The Wheel of Fortune, Ten of Swords.

DEATH.   ACE of SWORDS.   THE TOWER.   WHEEL of FORTUNE.

11. The Lovers accompanied by The Sun always testifies to a happy marriage.

THE LOVERS.   THE SUN.

12. The Lovers + The Empress (or Three of Swords) always testifies to sexual infidelity.

13. The Moon in reverse together with the Queen of Cups (or Queen of Pentacles) testifies to fertility problems.

14. The following cards testify to financial problems when two of them appear consecutively: Six of Pentacles, The Devil, Ten of Cups, Ten of Pentacles.

15. The Magician followed by the King of Swords in reverse or Judgement Day in reverse testifies to a legal problem.

16. The Star with Temperance testifies to a very easy-going character.

17. The Magician with any of the court cards in reverse testifies to sexual problems.

18. If on each side of The Lovers there is a card from the Major Arcana with women on it, this testifies to sexual attraction to women, if the querent is a woman, and to men, if the querent is a man.

19. The Chariot at the beginning or end of a spread indicates that the querent is confused and unfocused in everyday life.

20. The Hermit with Strength indicates a man who is dominated by his wife (even when the querent is a woman).

21. The combination of The Tower with one of the Swords cards or with The Moon testifies to a medical problem suffered by either the querent or someone close to him — a problem that clouds his life.

22. When two or more Knights appear consecutively, only the first of them to be revealed is taken into account. When the Knights do not appear consecutively in the spread, each one is considered individually.

23. In every case of the appearance of a number 7 card, it acts as a "trigger," that is, it activates the cards around it.

24. In every case of the appearance of a number 2 card, it slows down the action of the other cards; if two number 2 cards appear consecutively, they cancel the action of the rest of the cards.

25. When there is a combination of 6 and 8, the querent will be successful in his love life. When there is a combination in which 8 precedes 6, the querent will be unsuccessful in his love life.

26. When a person extracts the card which is parallel to his astrological sign, it is imperative to combine the astrological interpretation with that of the Tarot card.

27. Four of Swords + Six of Cups = stuck in the past.

28. Two of Swords + Six of Cups = frustrations from the past.

29. Three of Swords + Six of Cups = an injury from the past, which is still fresh.

30. Ace of Cups + Six of Cups = a new beginning with someone from the past.

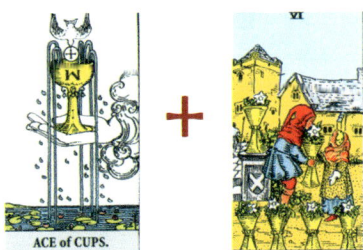

31. Seven of Cups + Four of Wands = a person who uses his imagination and reaps success and money. It could be an artist or an actor.

32. Seven of Pentacles = people live on a "back burner" and do not develop.

33. Eight of Wands + Five of Pentacles = gambler.

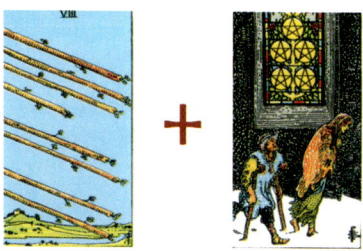

34. Eight of Wands + a card belonging to Sagittarius = a person who cannot be relied on.

35. Ace of Cups + Ten of Cups = a wedding, a common residence, and the purchase of a home together.

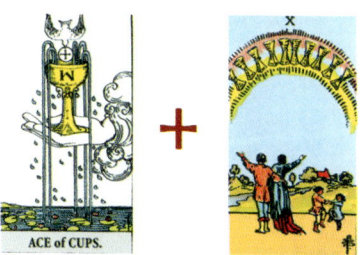

36. Eight of Wands + Four of Cups + Ten of Swords = you will extricate yourself from your problems

37. Ten of Swords + Six of Pentacles = failure, but gradual recovery.

38. Ten of Swords + Seven of Swords = failure without learning a lesson.

39. Three of Wands + a card belonging to Sagittarius = a trip abroad.

40. Three of Wands + Two of Wands = a trip abroad.

41. Thee of Cups + Four of Wands = a successful pregnancy.

42. Nine of Pentacles + Ace of Pentacles = a win at gambling.

43. The Magician + The Sun = a person who gets things done.

44. The Magician + The Chariot = there is understanding, but one has to attain self-control.

45. The Magician + The Star = strong mediumistic skills.

46. The High Priestess + The Hermit = spiritual isolation.

47. The High Priestess + The Empress = excessive emotionalism possibly leading to a loss of control.

48. The High Priestess + The Fool = naïvety and excessive emotional trust.

49. The Empress + The Emperor = success and material abundance.

50. The Emperor + The Fool = idealist, people place their trust in him.

51. The Emperor + Justice = obstinacy and tyranny.

52. The Emperor + The Sun = charisma, leadership ability, and doing things that will succeed and be implemented.

53. The Emperor + The Hanged Man = giving up on the ego.

54. The Hierophant + The Fool + The Magician = receives guidance from above, will reach an unexpected solution.

55. The Hierophant + The Empress = a compassionate and merciful father.

56. The Hierophant + The Sun = a religious functionary.

57. The Hierophant + The Hanged Man = a spiritual teacher without an ego.

58. The Hierophant + The Lovers = a positive choice.

59. The Hierophant + The Emperor = religious authority.

60. The Hierophant + Strength = of strong spiritual influence.

61. The Hierophant + The Star = inventive talent and brilliant ideas, but still not able to be implemented.

62. The Lovers + The Moon = a danger of distortion of the truth and a bad choice.

63. The Lovers + The World = many alternative possibilities, the choice will be easy.

64. The Lovers + The Tower = a mistaken choice that will lead to failure.

65. The Chariot + The Hermit = you will have to devote yourself to one thing only.

66. The Chariot + The Tower = an extremely dangerous gamble — either you will win or you will lose everything.

67. The Chariot + The Fool = more luck than sense.

68. The Chariot + The World = tough measures will not be necessary.

69. The Chariot + The Sun = creativity and spontaneity.

70. The Chariot + Justice = the moment of truth has come, you have to decide, even make a clean break.

71. The Chariot + The Empress = being carried away childishly.

72. Strength + The Hanged Man = total self-control.

73. Strength + Death = the desire to bend reality by force.

74. Strength + The Fool = power without sense.

75. The Hermit + Strength = the power to concentrate all one's efforts and move mountains. Determination in deciding.

76. The Hermit + The Tower = failure because you believe in yourself too much.

77. The Hermit + The Star = one's own spiritual path.

78. The Hermit + The Sun = stupidity, independence in one's opinions.

79. The Hermit + The Fool = stupidity, you believe in yourself too much.

80. The Hermit + The Empress = seeks to invest in one thing only, seeks one true love.

81. The Wheel of Fortune + The Hermit = awaits the opportune moment.

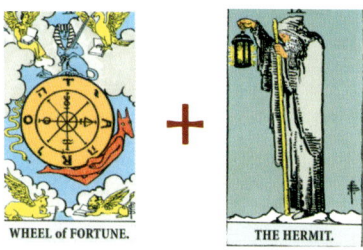

82. The Wheel of Fortune + The Magician = despite all the knowledge and skill, a surprise is expected.

83. The Wheel of Fortune + The Tower = failure as a result of external circumstances.

84. The Wheel of Fortune + The Fool = total lack of control.

85. Justice + The Hermit = isolation and total cutting off.

86. Justice + The Hanged Man = giving up on ego for the sake of adhering to the spiritual.

87. Justice + The Tower = you are liable to fail because of hesitancy; stop sitting on the fence.

88. Justice + The Fool = loosen up, stop being tense.

89. Justice + Strength = a huge effort, danger.

90. Justice + The Emperor = tyrant, stubborn, no point trying to talk to him.

91. The Hanged Man + The Empress = abundance of emotion and kindness.

92. The Hanged Man + Justice = exceptional powers of judgment without bias.

93. The Hanged Man + The Moon = lack of self-awareness.

94. The Hanged Man + The Sun = a person who is willing to work for the common good selflessly.

95. The Hanged Man + The Fool = inertia and indecision, waits for the world to come to him.

96. Death + The Moon = inner conflict.

97. Death + The Magician = a strong, unconscious tendency toward spiritual change.

98. Death + Justice = an extreme need for change.

99. Temperance + The Magician = exceptional spiritual wisdom.

100. Temperance + The Emperor = good diplomat, quiet person.

101. Temperance + The Empress = natural intuition, the ability to convey messages.

102. The Devil + The Fool = deceives himself and others with his stupidity.

103. The Devil + The Empress = attracted to black magic.

104. The Devil + The Emperor = control by means of intrigue.

105. The Devil + Justice = premeditated attempt to lead others astray.

106. Nine of Pentacles + Ace of Pentacles = participate in a lottery or sports gambles. There is a chance that you will win.

What it means when cards recur in spreads

In the following list, you can find tips for card-reading that relate not to the cards themselves, but to their position (upright or reverse) in the spread, or combinations of cards of the same number (from the Minor Arcana) in the spread. You can apply these tips to any spread types.

Upright:

If four knights appear in a spread, it is an indication of issues of great weight.

If three knights appear in a spread, it refers to a lively discussion about a controversial topic.

If two knights appear in a spread, it is a sign of intimacy.

KNIGHT of CUPS. KNIGHT of WANDS. KNIGHT of PENTACLES. KNIGHT of SWORDS.

In reverse:

If four knights appear in a spread, it is an indication of an alliance.

If three knights appear in a spread, it refers to a some kind of meeting or conflict — even physical.

If two knights appear in a spread, it is a sign of gullibility.

 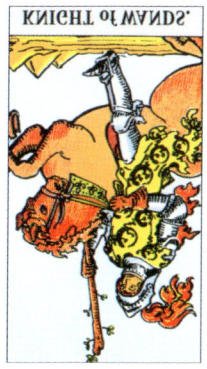  

Upright:

If four kings appear in a spread, it is a sign of prodigious honor.

If three kings appear in a spread, it refers to consultation.

If two kings appear in a spread, it is a matter of low-level advice.

In reverse:

If four kings appear in a spread, it is a sign of nimbleness.

If three kings appear in a spread, it refers to financial matters.

If two kings appear in a spread, it is a matter of things planned.

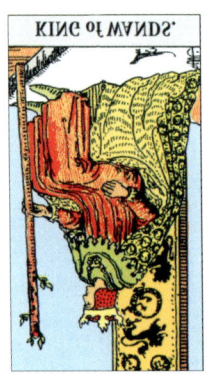

Upright:

If four queens appear in a spread, it is a sign of great controversy.

If three queens appear in a spread, it refers to female treachery.

If two queens appear in a spread, it is an indication of true friends.

In reverse:

If four queens appear in a spread, it is a warning about unsavory companions.

If three queens appear in a spread, it refers to gluttonous behavior.

If two queens appear in a spread, it is a reference to work.

Upright:

If four pages appear in a spread, it is a warning of a serious disease.

If three pages appear in a spread, it augurs a quarrel.

If two pages appear in a spread, it is a sign of unrest.

In reverse:

If four pages appear in a spread, it predicts privation.

If three pages appear in a spread, it refers to sloth.

If two pages appear in a spread, it is a sign of company.

 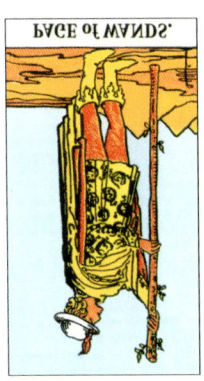  

Upright:

If four tens appear in a spread, it is a sign of an indictment.

If three tens appear in a spread, it is an indication of a completely changed situation.

If two tens appear in a spread, it is a sign of change.

   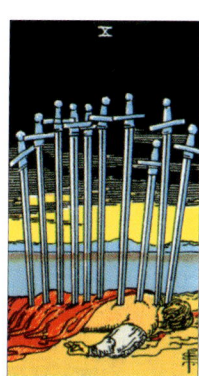

In reverse:

If four tens appear in a spread, it refers to an upcoming occasion or function.

If three tens appear in a spread, it is an indication of a disappointment.

If two tens appear in a spread, it means that something the querent anticipated has actually happened.

Upright:

If four nines appear in a spread, it refers to a loyal comrade.

If three nines appear in a spread, it is a sign of success.

If two nines appear in a spread, it means that the querent will receive something.

In reverse:

If four nines appear in a spread, it refers to exaggerated interest on a loan.

If three nines appear in a spread, it is a sign of injudicious behavior.

If two nines appear in a spread, it means that the querent will make a minor profit.

   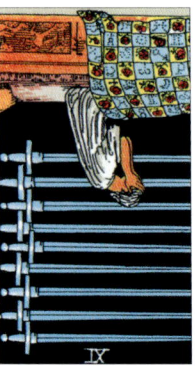

Upright:

If four eights appear in a spread, it is a sign of adversity.

If three eights appear in a spread, it indicates marriage.

If two eights appear in a spread, it refers to the acquisition of knowledge.

 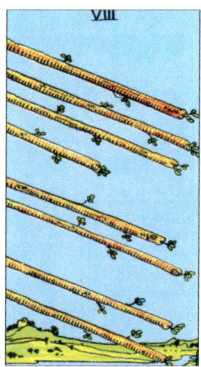  

In reverse:

If four eights appear in a spread, it refers to a mistake.

If three eights appear in a spread, it refers to an unforgettable sight.

If two eights appear in a spread, it is an indication of vicissitudes.

Upright:

If four sevens appear in a spread, it is a sign of conniving and mystery.

If three sevens appear in a spread, it indicates a poor state of health.

If two sevens appear in a spread, it is a prediction of imminent tidings.

In reverse:

If four sevens appear in a spread, it refers to people involved in a dispute.

If three sevens appear in a spread, it is an indication of happiness.

If two sevens appear in a spread, it refers to women whose reputations are neither good nor bad.

   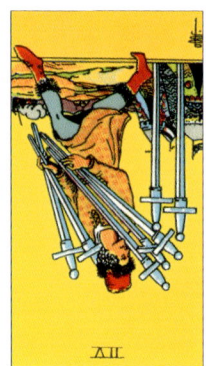

Upright:

If four sixes appear in a spread, it indicates plenty.

If three sixes appear in a spread, it refers to success.

If two sixes appear in a spread, it warns of irascibility.

In reverse:

If four sixes appear in a spread, it indicates concern.

If three sixes appear in a spread, it refers to fulfillment.

If two sixes appear in a spread, it warns of a fall from a lofty position.

Upright:

If four fives appear in a spread, it is a sign of constancy.

If three fives appear in a spread, it is an indication of determination.

If two fives appear in a spread, it predicts keeping watch.

In reverse:

If four fives appear in a spread, it is a sign of good organization.

If three fives appear in a spread, it is an indication of vacillation.

If two fives appear in a spread, it predicts adversity.

Upright:

If four fours appear in a spread, it is an indication of an imminent trip.

If three fours appear in a spread, it means that the querent has something to ponder about.

If two fours appear in a spread, it warns of sleeplessness.

   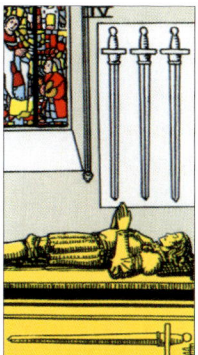

In reverse:

If four fours appear in a spread, it is an indication of a hike outdoors.

If three fours appear in a spread, it refers to anxiety.

If two fours appear in a spread, it warns of a quarrel.

   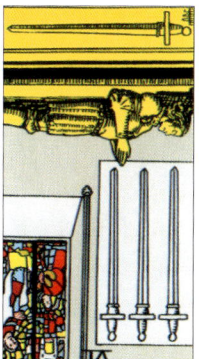

Upright:

If four threes appear in a spread, it is a sign of advancement.

If three threes appear in a spread, it refers to a sense of oneness.

If two threes appear in a spread, it predicts serenity.

In reverse:

If four threes appear in a spread, it is a sign of huge success.

If three threes appear in a spread, it refers to a sense of tranquillity.

If two threes appear in a spread, it predicts security.

   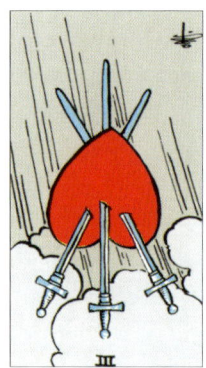

Upright:

If four twos appear in a spread, it is an indication of dissent.

If three twos appear in a spread, it refers to a secure feeling.

If two twos appear in a spread, it is a sign of harmony.

In reverse:

If four twos appear in a spread, it refers to making up after a disagreement.

If three twos appear in a spread, it warns of worry.

If two twos appear in a spread, it is a sign of suspicion.

Upright:

If four aces appear in a spread, it is a sign of potential luck.

If three aces appear in a spread, it means that the querent will enjoy a minor triumph.

If two aces appear in a spread, it warns the querent against being taken for a ride.

ACE of CUPS.

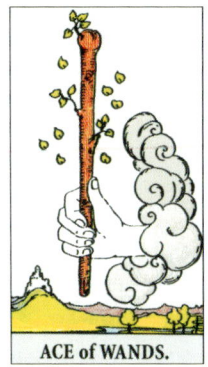
ACE of WANDS.

ACE of PENTACLES.

ACE of SWORDS.

In reverse:

If four aces appear in a spread, it is a sign of disgrace.

If three aces appear in a spread, it refers to lecherous conduct.

If two aces appear in a spread, it warns the querent of adversaries.

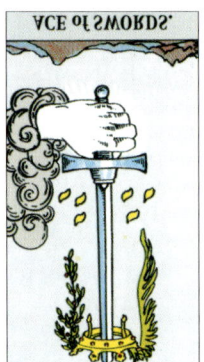

Arthur Waite's Tips

When Waite published his Tarot deck, he also published a booklet in which he provided key sentences for each card. Below, we present a synopsis of those sentences for all 78 cards.

1. The Magician

You must exercise tact in the near future. It would be good for you to display your skills. Your self-confidence will serve you well.
In reverse: Watch out for situations that could lead to mental breakdowns and other illnesses.

2. The High Priestess

Your future is full of mystery. Your persistence and intelligence will play an important role in the future. Do not waste words — remember that silence is golden.
In reverse: Watch out for the dangers of vanity and superficiality.

3. The Empress

You will be required to display initiative and resourcefulness in the future. You may have to cope with uncertainty and a lack of knowledge.
In reverse: You will solve complicated issues, and this will help you reach the truth and gain enlightenment.

4. The Emperor

In the future, you will enjoy a solid basis and high standing. You can feel free from threat and danger.
In reverse: Try to behave with kindness and empathy.

5. The Hierophant

You can expect to form some kind of relationship, such as marriage or a partnership, in the future. You will have a chance to display your innate compassion and good nature.
In reverse: Your astuteness will stand you in good stead in days to come.
Don't let people take advantage of your good nature — it will make you appear weak.

6. The Lovers

Love and passion await you in the future. You will triumph over the obstacles in your path.
In reverse: If you don't act cautiously, you will not succeed in either your plans or your relationship.

7. The Chariot

You will be helped in the future — possibly by a more powerful force than your fellow human beings.
Be careful not to fall into the trap of seeking revenge.
In reverse: You are warned about serious conflicts — even physical battles — and bitter defeats.

8. Fortitude

You will have the opportunity of displaying your positive attributes, such as your ability to take action and to work energetically.
You will be successful in the future.
In reverse: Don't let power go to your head; if you abuse it, you run the risk of a rapid downfall and shame.

9. The Hermit

You must act cautiously and tactfully in the future. Watch out for other people's betrayal and two-faced conduct.
In reverse: If you do not act in a straightforward manner, you will be haunted by anxiety. Don't hide behind false appearances.

10. Wheel of Fortune

The future holds a lot of good fortune and happiness for you.
You can expect a rise in your status.
In reverse: You can look forward to a life of plenty — be careful that you don't become wasteful.

11. Justice

Your talents for balanced judgment will come to the fore in the future. If you are involved in legal proceedings, you will win the case.

In reverse: Watch out for the long arm of the law — it can embroil you in complications you never dreamed of.

12. The Hanged Man

You must concentrate on your powers of prediction and soothsaying.

In reverse: Don't give in to egoistic inclinations. You must take care not to be swept along by the opinion of the majority.

13. Death

You must watch out for your interests; there are people who seek your downfall and ruin. If you are a woman, you will have to deal with many problems. If you are an unmarried woman, you may suffer a disappointment in love.

In reverse: You will have to face the challenge of inactivity and apathy. There may be a disappointment in the future.

14. Temperance

You will have the chance to show your ability to save money and live frugally in the future. Your management abilities will come to the fore.

In reverse: You will be exposed to things concerning religion and religious functionaries.

15. The Devil

Be on the lookout for damage and violence in the future. You will display your abilities to make superhuman efforts and be extremely emphatic.

In reverse: Be careful of petty, nit-picking behavior in the future. You may encounter a situation in which you have to force yourself to be strong.

16. The Tower

You will have to take great care in the future if you want to avoid the unexpected calamities and hardships this card represents.

In reverse: You can expect similar, if slightly less serious, events.

17. The Star

The future holds two possible directions for you — one is full of hope and opportunity, while the other contains negative things such as burglary, loss, and abandonment.

In reverse: You must refrain from overbearing and condescending behavior.

18. The Moon

There are perils and treachery awaiting the hapless querent in the future. Be alert and fearless in order to avoid the forces of evil and darkness.

In reverse: Watch out for other people who want to undermine your stability through betrayal and misrepresentation.

19. The Sun

You will be prosperous and content in the future.

In reverse: A slightly lesser degree of the same prediction.

20. Judgment

You will get a new job in the future. It is good for you to begin a process of self-renewal.

In reverse: Do not let cowardice and weakness ruin your chances in the future.

21. The World

You will definitely be successful in the future — and you will be rewarded for this. You will travel extensively, and may even decide to live in another country.

In reverse: Try not to succumb to apathy. If you think and act positively, you will avoid getting into a rut.

22. The Fool

In the future, you must guard yourself from extremes of emotions leading to profligacy, madness, and manic behavior.

In reverse: Let your conduct be normal and rational in the future, and not completely devoid of caring and involvement. See that your attitude toward others is not one of condescension.

The Cups Suit

Knight
A friend will visit you and, as a result, you will receive an unanticipated sum of money.

Seven
This card indicates a lovely child, as well as plans and decisions.
In reverse: It sometimes indicates success.

King
Somebody in authority may decide to make your life difficult. Watch out for insincere offers of assistance.
In reverse: This card is a sign of loss.

Six
This card represents happy reminiscences.
In reverse: There could be a sudden bequest.

Queen
This can be an indication of a spurious nature.
In reverse: This card points to marriage — wealthy brides and distinguished grooms.

Five
This is a good card in the main, indicating a good marriage, as well as money in the form of bequests and gifts.
In reverse: You may be surprised by the unexpected return of a long-lost relative.

Page
This card foretells positive things.
In reverse: This card foretells negative things.

Four
This card indicates vicissitudes.
In reverse: You may have a feeling about something about to happen.

Ten
A man can expect to marry surprisingly well.
In reverse: This card indicates sadness and disputes.

Three
A person in the armed forces may get an unanticipated promotion.
In reverse: This card promises healing, closure, and comfort.

Nine
People in the armed forces can expect good tidings with this card.
In reverse: You will be successful in business.

Two
This card augurs well in the realms of romance, business, pleasure, status, and finance.
In reverse: You will undergo passionate experiences.

Eight
You will marry a good-looking person.
In reverse: Your happiness will be complete.

Ace
You will encounter a will of steel and realize that the law cannot be bent.
In reverse: You may be surprised when someone else changes his tack.

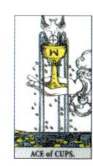

The Wands Suit

Knight
This card does not promise positive things, but you should make every effort to remain within the fold.
In reverse: It could mean marriage — but not necessarily a happy one.

Seven
This card concerns children.

King
This card is mainly positive, often indicating a successful marriage.
In reverse:
You should take the advice offered.

Six
Employers may no longer trust their employees. The card indicates deception.
In reverse: Long-forgotten hopes may finally be fulfilled.

Queen
The results of things you have initiated will be good.
In reverse:
You are well liked, but this may not be of assistance to you.

Five
You can expect a gamble to come off profitably.
In reverse:
A dispute may lead to something good.

Page
This is the "dating" card.
In reverse:
This card does not bring particularly good tidings.

Four
You will have good luck that you never dreamed of.
In reverse:
You can expect to have lovely children.

Ten
This card can indicate hardships and misunderstandings — it depends where it falls in the spread.

Three
This is an excellent card. It indicates that working together with someone else will yield dividends.

Nine
This is not the best card.

Two
You may experience some minor letdowns.

Eight
You can expect a rough patch with your spouse.

Ace
This card foretells all kinds of disasters.
In reverse: A baby will be born.